STEPS TOWARDS HEAVEN

STEPS TOWARDS HEAVEN

J. C. Ryle

THE BANNER OF TRUTH TRUST

THE BANNER OF TRUTH TRUST
3 Murrayfield Road, Edinburgh EH12 6EL, UK
P.O. Box 621, Carlisle, PA 17013, USA

*

© Banner of Truth Trust 2017

ISBN
Print: 978 1 84871 696 4
EPUB: 978 1 84871 698 8
Kindle: 978 1 84871 699 5

*

Typeset in 11/15 Adobe Garamond Pro at
The Banner of Truth Trust, Edinburgh

Printed in the USA by
Versa Press, Inc.,
East Peoria, IL

Contents

Publisher's Preface

THE five chapters that make up this little book are drawn from a larger work compiled by J. C. Ryle and first published in 1877 under the title *Old Paths*. The chapters were among a number of papers or tracts that set forth 'the leading truths of Christianity which are "necessary to salvation"'.

It is interesting that Ryle thought it necessary that such a book should be published in the last quarter of the nineteenth century at a time when Christianity *appeared* to occupy such a prominent place in the English-speaking world. Yet, even in Ryle's day, there was great confusion about the 'way to heaven'.

Ryle's book is a good indication that, in some respects at least, little has changed during the last 140 years since its pages first saw the light of day. Then, as now, the gospel of Jesus Christ was frequently misunderstood. For example, it was widely believed that one could be 'saved' without any personal knowledge of the great truths taught in the Bible. Then, as now, many voices were raised against any need of clarity of thought or precision in doctrine regarding the essence of the Christian gospel. In the nineteenth century, just as in the twenty-first, there were many who believed that God's love is such that no one will ultimately suffer eternal loss of body and soul.

One of the great ironies that strikes us as we look back to the period in which Ryle lived is that this man who advocated 'simple, unadulterated, old-fashioned Evangelical theology' is today widely read all around the world, while those who advocated the forsaking of the 'old paths' and the adoption of new and exciting ways of thinking are now forgotten; their 'ground-breaking' works, once so fashionable, lie unwanted, unloved, and unread under thick layers of dust on gloomy library shelves. Why should that be the case? Why is it that Ryle's writings have stood the test of time and continue to appeal to readers more than a century after his death? The answer, in large part, lies in his own words: 'for *real* inward effects on hearts and outward effects on lives, I see no teaching so powerful as thorough, genuine Evangelical teaching'.

This book perhaps should come with a 'spiritual health warning'. The living God may well use it to change the reader on the *inside* (one's heart) and on the *outside* (the way one lives). Within its pages vitally important truths are clearly explained and forcefully applied—truths about *Sin, Salvation, Conversion, Justification,* and *the Holy Spirit's work*. The author (on account of his faithfulness to the teaching of the Bible) will help to dispel the darkness of misunderstanding and bring the reader into the light of God's truth. Above all, he will leave the reader in no doubt that *real* Christianity is the outworking of a supernatural work of the Spirit of God in the human soul.

I

Our Sins

Make me to know my transgression and my sin.—Job 13:23.
Our sins testify against us.—Isa. 59:12.
Cleanse me from my sin.—Psa. 51:2.
The blood of Jesus Christ his Son cleanseth us from all sin.
   —1 John 1:7.

THE two words which head this page ought to stir up within us great searchings of heart. They concern every man and woman born into the world. To know 'our sins' is the first letter in the alphabet of saving religion. To understand our position in the sight of God is one step towards heaven. The true secret of peace of conscience is to feel 'our sins' put away. If we love life we ought never to rest till we can give a satisfactory answer to the question,—'WHERE ARE MY SINS?'

I ask my readers this day to look this simple question in the face. A time draws nigh when the question *must* be answered. The hour cometh when all other questions will seem like a drop of water in comparison with this. We shall not say, 'Where is my money?'—or, 'Where are my lands?'—or, 'Where is my property?' Our only thought will be, 'My sins! my sins!—Where are my sins?'

I am going to offer a few remarks which may help to throw light on the mighty subject which is before our eyes. My heart's desire and prayer to God is this,—that this paper may be useful to the souls of all who read this volume. I entreat you to give it a fair reading. Read it: read it! Read it to the end! Who can tell but the Holy Ghost may employ this paper for the saving of your soul?

I. My first remark is this. *You have many sins.*

I say this boldly, and without the least hesitation. I know not who you are, or how the time past of your life has been spent. But I know, from the Word of God, that every son and daughter of Adam is a great sinner in the sight of God. There is no exception: it is the common disease of the whole family of mankind in every quarter of the globe. From the king on his throne, to the beggar by the roadside,—from the landlord in his hall, to the labourer in his cottage,—from the fine lady in her drawing-room, to the humblest maid-servant in the kitchen,—from the clergyman in the pulpit, to the little child in the Sunday school,—we are all by nature guilty, guilty, guilty in the sight of God. 'In many things we offend all.'—'There is none righteous: no, not one.'—'All have sinned.'—'If we say that we have no sin, we deceive ourselves, and the truth is not in us' (James 3:2;

Rom. 3:10; 5:12; 1 John 1:8). It is useless to deny it. We have all sinned many sins!

Does anyone doubt the truth of these words? Then go and examine *the law of God*, as expounded by the Son of God himself. Read with attention the fifth chapter of St Matthew's Gospel. See how the commandments of God apply to our words as well as to our actions, and to our thoughts and motives, as well as to our words. Know that 'the Lord seeth not as man seeth: man looketh at the outward appearance, but the Lord looketh at the heart.' In his sight the very 'thought of foolishness is sin' (1 Sam. 16:7; Prov. 24:9).

And now turn to the history of *your own life*, and try it by the standard of this holy law. Think of the days of your childhood, and all your waywardness, and selfishness, and evil tempers, and perversity, and backwardness to that which is good.—Remember the days of your youth,—your self-will, your pride, your worldly inclinations, your impatience of control, your longing after forbidden things.—Call to mind your conduct since you came to man's estate, and the many departures from the right way, of which you have been guilty every year.—Surely, in the face of your life's history, you will not stand up and say, 'I have not sinned!'

And then turn to the history of *your own heart*. Consider how many evil things have gone through it, of which the world knows nothing at all.—Remember the thousands of sinful imaginations, and corrupt ideas, which your heart has entertained, even while your outward conduct has been correct, moral, and respectable.—Think of the vile thoughts, and deceitful intentions, and false motives, and malicious, envious, spiteful feelings, which have walked up and down in your inward man, while those nearest to you never dreamed or guessed what was going on.—Surely, in the face of your heart's history, you will not stand up and say, 'I have not sinned!'

Once more I ask every reader of this paper, Do you doubt what I am saying? Do you doubt whether you have sinned many sins?—Then go and examine the twenty-fifth chapter of St Matthew's Gospel. Read the concluding portion of that chapter, which describes the proceedings of the *judgment day*. Note carefully the grounds on which the wicked, at the left hand, are condemned to everlasting fire. No mention is made of great open acts of wickedness which they have committed. They are not charged with having murdered, or stolen, or borne false witness, or committed adultery. They are condemned for *sins of omission*! The mere fact that they have left undone things which they ought to have done, is sufficient to ruin their souls for ever. In short, a man's sins of omission alone are enough to sink him into hell!

And now look at yourself by the light of this wonderful passage of Scripture. Try to remember the countless things you have left undone, which you might have done, and have left unsaid, that you might have said. The acts of self-denying kindness, which you might have performed, but have neglected,—how many they are! The good you might have done, and the happiness you might have caused, at very little trouble to yourself,—how vast is the amount of it! Surely, in the face of our Lord's teaching about sins of omission, you will not stand up and say, 'I have not sinned!'

Once more I ask, Do you doubt the truth of what I am saying? I think it quite possible that you do. As a minister of Christ for more than a quarter of a century, I know something of man's exceeding blindness to his own natural state. Listen to me once more, whilst I ply your conscience with another argument. Oh, that God may open your eyes, and show you what you are!

Sit down, and take pen and paper, and count up the sins that you have probably sinned since you first knew good from evil. Sit down, I say, and *make a sum*. Grant for a moment that there have been on an average, fifteen hours in every twenty-four during which you have been awake, and an active and accountable being. Grant for a moment that in each one of these fifteen hours you have sinned only two sins. Surely you will not say that this is an unfair supposition. Remember we may sin against God in thought, word, or deed. I repeat, it cannot be thought an extreme thing to suppose that in each waking hour of your life you have, in thought, or word, or deed, sinned two sins. And now add up the sins of your life, and see to what sum they will amount.

At the rate of fifteen waking hours in a day, you have sinned every day thirty sins!—At the rate of seven days in a week, you have sinned two hundred and ten sins every week!—At the rate of four weeks in every mouth, you have sinned eight hundred and forty sins every month!—At the rate of twelve months in every year, you have sinned ten thousand and eighty sins every year!—And, in short, not to go further with the calculation, every ten years of your life you have sinned, at the lowest computation, more than ONE HUNDRED THOUSAND SINS!

I invite you to look calmly at this sum. I defy you to disprove its correctness. I ask you, on the contrary, whether I have not entirely understated your case? I appeal to you, as an honest person, whether it be not true, that many an hour, and many a day in your life, you have sinned incessantly? I ask you confidently, whether the sum would not be far more correct if the total number of your sins was multiplied ten-fold?—Oh, cease from your self-righteousness! Lay aside this proud affectation of 'not being so very bad', in which you are trying to wrap yourself up. Be bold enough to confess the truth. Listen not to that old liar, the devil. Surely in the face of that damning sum which I have just cast up, you will not dare to deny that 'you have many sins'.

I leave this part of my subject here, and pass on. I sadly fear that many a reader will run his eye over what I have been saying, and remain unconvinced and unmoved. I have learned by mournful experience that the last thing man finds out and understands, is his own state in the sight of God. Well saith the Holy Ghost, that we are all by nature 'blind', and 'deaf', and 'dumb', and 'asleep', and 'beside ourselves', and 'dead'! Nothing, nothing will ever convince man of sin but the power of the Holy Ghost. Show him hell, and he will not flee from it; show him heaven, and he will not seek it; silence him with warnings, and yet he will not stir; prick his conscience, and yet he will remain hard. Power from on high must come down and do the work. To show man what he really is, is the special work of the Holy Spirit of God.

He that has any feeling of his own sinfulness, ought to thank God for it. That very sense of weakness, wickedness, and corruption, which perhaps makes you uncomfortable, is in reality a token for good, and a cause for praise. The first step towards being really good, is to feel *bad*. The first preparation for heaven, is to know that we deserve nothing but *hell*. Before we can be counted righteous we must know ourselves to be miserable *sinners*. Before we can have inward happiness and peace with God, we must learn to be ashamed and confounded because of our manifold transgressions. Before we can rejoice in a well-grounded hope, we must be taught to say, 'Unclean: unclean! God, be merciful to me a sinner!'

He that really loves his own soul must beware of checking and stifling this inward feeling of sinfulness. I beseech you, by the mercies of God, do not trample on it, do not crush it, do not take it by the throat and refuse to give it your attention. Beware of taking the advice of worldly men about it. Treat it not as a case of low-spirits, disordered health, or anything of the kind. Beware of listening to the devil's counsel about it. Do not try to drown it in drink and revelling; do not try to drive over it with horses, and dogs, and carriages, and field-sports; do not try to purge it away by a course of card-parties, and balls, and concerts. Oh, if you love your soul, do not, do not treat the first sense of sin in this miserable fashion! Do not commit spiritual suicide,—do not murder your soul!

Go rather and pray God to show you what this feeling of sin means. Ask him to send the Holy Spirit to teach you what you are, and what he would have you to do. Go and read your Bible, and see whether there is not just cause for your being uncomfortable, and whether this sense of being 'wicked and bad' is not just what you have a right to expect. Who can tell but it is a seed from heaven, which is one day to bear fruit in Paradise in your complete salvation? Who can tell but it is a spark from heaven, which God means to blow up into a steady and shining fire? Who can tell but it is a little stone from above, before which the devil's kingdom in your heart is to go down, and a stone which shall prove the first foundation of a glorious temple of the Holy Ghost?—Happy indeed is that man or woman who can go along with my first remark, and say, 'IT IS TRUE. I HAVE MANY SINS.'

II. My second remark is this. *It is of the utmost importance to have our sins taken off us and put away.*

I say this boldly and confidently. I am aware of the multitude of things which are thought 'important' in the world, and receive the first and best of men's attentions. But I know well what I am saying. I am bold to say that my Master's business deserves to be placed before all other business; and I learn from my Master's book that there is nothing of such importance to a man as to have his sins forgiven and cleansed away.

Let us remember *there is a God above us.* We see him not in the city. Hurry and bustle, trade and commerce, appear to swallow up men's minds. We see him not in the country. Farming and labouring go on in regular course, and seed time and harvest never fail. But all this time there is an eternal Eye looking down from heaven and seeing all that men do: an eye that never slumbers, and never sleeps. Yes! there is not only a queen, and a government, and a landlord, and a master, and an employer, to be remembered. There is One higher, far higher than all these, who expects his dues to be paid. That One is the Most High God.

This God is a God of infinite *holiness.* He is of 'purer eyes than to behold evil, and canst not look on iniquity' (Hab. 1:13). He sees defects and infirmities where we see none. In his sight the very 'heavens are not clean' (Job 15:15). He is a God of infinite *knowledge.* He knows every thought, and word, and action of every one of Adam's children: there are no secrets hid from him. All that we think, and say, and do, is noted down and recorded in the book of his remembrance.—He is a God of infinite *power*. He made all things at the beginning. He orders all things according to his will. He casts down the kings of this world in a moment. None can stand against him when he is angry.—Above all, he is a God in whose hands are our lives and all our concerns. He first gave us being. He has kept us alive since we were born. He will remove us when he sees fit, and reckon with us according to our ways. Such is the God with whom we have to do.

Let us think of these things. Surely, as Job says, 'when you consider you will be afraid' (Job 23:15). Surely you will see it is of the utmost importance to have your sins cleansed away. Surely you will inquire, 'How do matters stand between me and God?'

Let us remember, furthermore, that *death is before us.* We cannot live always. There must be an end, one day, of all our scheming and planning, and buying and selling, and working and toiling. A visitor will come to our house who will take no denial. The king of terrors will demand admission, and serve us with notice to quit. Where are the rulers and kings who governed millions a hundred years ago? Where are the rich men who made fortunes and founded houses? Where are the landlords who received rents and added field to field? Where are the labourers who ploughed the land and reaped the corn? Where are the clergymen who read services and preached sermons? Where are the children who played in the sunshine as if they would never be old? Where are the old men who leaned on their sticks and gossiped about 'the days when they were young'? There is but one answer. They are all dead, dead, dead! Strong, and beautiful, and active as they once were, they are all dust and ashes now. Mighty and important as they all thought their business, it all came to an end. And we are travelling in the same way! A few more years and we also shall be lying in our graves!

Let us think of these things. Surely when you consider your latter end you will not think the cleansing away of sin a light matter. Surely you will see something in the question, 'Where are your sins?' Surely you will consider, 'How am I going to die?'

Let us remember, furthermore, that *resurrection and judgment await us*. All is not over when the last breath is drawn and our bodies become a lump of cold clay. No: all is not over! The realities of existence then begin. The shadows will have passed away for ever. The trumpet shall one day sound, and call us forth from our narrow bed. The graves shall be rent asunder, and their tenants shall be summoned forth to meet God. The ears that would not obey the church-going bell shall be obliged to obey another summons; the proud wills that would not submit to listen to sermons shall be compelled to listen to the judgment of God. The great white throne shall be set: the books shall be opened. Every man, woman, and child, shall be arraigned at that great assize. Everyone shall be judged according to his works. The sins of everyone shall be answered for. And everyone shall receive his eternal portion either in heaven or in hell!

Let us think of these things. Surely in remembrance of that day you must allow that the subject I am upon deserves attention. Surely you must confess that it is of the utmost importance to have your sins cleansed away. Surely you will consider, 'How am I going to be judged?'

I must speak out what is upon my mind. I feel great sorrow and trouble of heart about many men and women in the world. I fear for many who live in this so-called Christian land; I fear for many who profess and call themselves Christians; I fear for many who go to church or chapel every Sunday and have a decent form of religion; I fear that they do not see the immense importance of having their sins cleansed away. I can see plainly that there are many other things which they think far more *important*. Money, and land, and farms, and horses, and carriages, and dogs, and meat, and drink, and clothes, and houses, and marriages, and families, and business, and pleasure,—these, these are the sort of things which many evidently think the 'first things'. And as for the forgiveness and cleansing away of their sins, it is a matter which has only the second place in their thoughts.

See the man of business, as he pores over his ledger and account books, and runs his eye over the columns of figures.

See the man of pleasure, as he tears over the country with his horses and dogs, or rushes after excitement at the races, the theatre, the card party, or the ball. See the poor thoughtless labourer, as he carries off his hard-earned wages to the public house, and wastes them in ruining both body and soul. See them all, how thoroughly they are in earnest! See them all, how they throw their hearts into what they are doing!—And then mark them all at church next Sunday: listless, careless, yawning, sleepy, and indifferent, as if there were no God, and no devil, and no Christ, and no heaven, and no hell! Mark how evident it is that they have left their hearts outside the church! Mark how plain it is that they have no real interest in religion! And then say whether it be not true that many know nothing of the importance of having their sins cleansed away. O, take heed lest this be the case with you!

Does any reader of these pages feel anything of the importance of being forgiven? Then, in the name of God, I call upon you to encourage that feeling more and more. This is the point to which we desire to bring all people's souls. We want you to understand that religion does not consist in professing certain opinions, and performing certain outward duties, and going through certain outward forms. It consists in being reconciled to God, and enjoying peace with him. It consists in having our sins cleansed away, and knowing that they are cleansed. It consists in being brought back into friendship with the King of kings, and living in the sunshine of that friendship.—Listen not to those who would fain persuade you that if you only 'go to church' regularly you will of course go to heaven. Settle it rather in your mind, that true saving religion, such as the Bible teaches, is another kind of thing altogether. The very foundation of real Christianity is to know that you have many sins, and deserve hell,—and to feel the importance of having these sins cleansed away, in order that you may go to heaven.

Happy, says the world, are they who have plenty of property and fine houses! Happy are they who have carriages, and horses, and servants, and large balances at their bankers, and great troops of friends! Happy are they who are clothed in purple and fine linen, and fare sumptuously every day, who have nothing to do but to spend their money and enjoy themselves!—Yet what is the real value of such happiness? It gives no solid, real satisfaction, even at the time of enjoyment. It endures but for a few years. It only lasts till death comes in, like the hand at Belshazzar's feast, and breaks up all. And then, in too many cases, this so-called happiness is exchanged for ETERNAL MISERY IN HELL.

'Blessed,' says the Word of God, 'are those whose iniquities are forgiven, and whose sins are covered! Blessed is the man unto whom the Lord imputeth not iniquity!—Blessed are the poor in spirit, for theirs is the kingdom of heaven! Blessed are they that mourn, for they shall be comforted! Blessed are they that hunger and thirst after righteousness, for they shall be filled!' (Psa. 32:1-2; Matt. 5:2, *etc.*).—Their blessedness shall never come to an end: their happiness is no summer dried fountain, just failing when need is the sorest; their friends are no summer swallows, forsaking them, like Adonijah's guests, the first moment that the trumpet sounds. Their sun shall never go down. Their joy shall bud in time, and bloom in eternity. Theirs, in a word, is true happiness, for it is *for evermore.*

Do you believe what I am saying? It is all scriptural and true. You will see one day whose words shall stand, the words of man or the Word of God. Be wise in time. Settle it in your heart this very hour, that the most important thing that man can attend to is the cleansing and forgiveness of his sins.

III. My third remark is this. *We cannot cleanse away our own sins.*

I make this statement boldly and confidently. Startling as it sounds to the natural heart, I lay it down as a piece of undeniable scriptural truth. In spite of all the Pharisees, and Roman Catholics, and Socinians, and Deists, and idolaters of human reason and human power, I unhesitatingly repeat my assertion.—Man's sins are many and great. It is of the utmost importance that these sins should be cleansed away. Man's guilt in the sight of God, is enormous. Man's danger of hell, after he dies, is imminent and tremendous. And yet man cannot cleanse away his own sins! It is written, and it is true, 'By the deeds of the law shall no flesh be justified' (Rom. 3:20).

(*a*) It will not cleanse away your sins *to be sorry for them*.

You may mourn over your past wickedness, and humble yourself in sackcloth and ashes. You may shed floods of tears, and acknowledge your own guilt and danger. You may—you must,—you ought to do this. But you will not by so doing wipe out your transgressions from the book of God. SORROW CANNOT MAKE ATONEMENT FOR SIN.

The convicted criminal in a court of justice is often sorry for his offences. He sees the misery and ruin they have brought upon him. He mourns over his folly in not listening to advice and in giving way to temptation. But the judge does not let him off because he is sorry. The deed has been done; the law has been broken; the penalty has been incurred. The punishment must be inflicted, notwithstanding the criminal's tears.—This is precisely your position in the sight of God. Your sorrow is right, and good, and proper. But your sorrow has no power whatever to cleanse away your sins. It needs something more than penitence to take the burden off your heart.

(*b*) It will not cleanse away your sins *to mend your life*: You may reform your conduct, and turn over a new leaf; you may break off many evil habits, and take up many good ones; you may become, in short, an altered man in all your outward behaviour. You may,—you must,—you ought to do so. Without such change no soul ever was saved. But you will not by so doing wipe away one particle of your guilt in God's sight. REFORMATION MAKES NO ATONEMENT FOR SIN.

The bankrupt tradesman, who owes ten thousand pounds and has not ten shillings to pay, may resolve to become a reformed character. After wasting his whole substance in riotous living he may become steady, temperate, and respectable. It is all right and proper that he should be so: but this will not satisfy the claims of those to whom he owes money. Once more I say, this is precisely your case by nature in the sight of God. You owe him ten thousand talents, and have 'nothing to pay'. Today's amendments are all very well, but they do not wipe away yesterday's debts.—It requires something more than amendment and reformation to give you a light heart and to set your conscience free.

(c) It will not cleanse away your sins to become *diligent in the use of the forms and ordinances of religion.* You may alter your habits about Sunday, and attend services from morning to night; you may take pains to hear preaching on week-days, as well as on Sundays; you may receive the Lord's supper on every possible occasion, and give alms, and keep fasts. It is all very well as far as it goes. It is a right and proper thing to attend to your religious duties. But all the means of grace in the world will never do you any good so long as you trust in them as saviours. They will not bind up the wounds of your heart, and give you inward peace. Formality cannot make atonement for sin.

A lantern on a dark night is a very useful thing. It can help the traveller to find his way home; it can preserve him from losing his path, and keep him from falling into danger.

But the lantern itself is not the traveller's fireside. The man who is content to sit down in the road by the side of his lantern, must never be surprised if he dies of cold. If you try to satisfy your conscience with a formal attendance on means of grace, you are no wiser than this traveller. It needs something more than religious formality to take the burden from your conscience and to give you peace with God.

(*d*) It will not cleanse away your sins *to look to man for help*. It is not in the power of any child of Adam to save another's soul. No bishop, no priest, no ordained man of any church or denomination has power to forgive sins: no human absolution, however solemnly conferred, can purge that conscience which is not purged by God. It is well to ask the counsel of the ministers of the gospel when the conscience is perplexed. It is their office to help the labouring and heavy laden, and to show them the way of peace. But it is not in the power of any minister to deliver any man from his guilt. We can only show the path that must be followed: we can only point out the door at which everyone must knock. It requires a hand far stronger than that of man to take the chains off conscience, and set the prisoner free. No CHILD OF ADAM CAN TAKE AWAY HIS BROTHER'S SINS.

The bankrupt who asks a bankrupt to set him up in business again is only losing time. The pauper who travels off to a neighbour pauper, and begs him to help him out of difficulties, is only troubling himself in vain. The prisoner does not beg his fellow-prisoner to set him free; the shipwrecked sailor does not call on his shipwrecked comrade to place him safe ashore. Help in all these cases must come from some other quarter: relief in all these cases must be sought from some other hand. It is just the same in the matter of cleansing away your sins. So long as you seek it from man, whether man ordained or man not ordained, you seek it where it cannot be found. You must go further: you must look higher. You must turn elsewhere for comfort. It is not in the power of any man on earth or in heaven to take the burden of sin from off another man's soul. 'None can by any means redeem his brother, nor give to God a ransom for him' (Psa. 49:7).

Thousands in every age have tried to cleanse themselves from their sins in the ways I have now described, and have tried in vain. Thousands, I doubt not, are trying at this very moment, and find themselves 'nothing bettered, but rather worse' (Mark 5:26). They are climbing up a steep precipice of ice, toiling hard, and yet slipping backwards as fast as they climb.—They are pouring water into a cask full of holes, labouring busily, and yet no nearer the end of their work than when they began.—They are rowing a boat against a rapid stream, plying the oar diligently, and yet in reality losing ground every minute.—They are trying to build up a wall of loose sand, wearing themselves out with fatigue, and yet seeing their work roll down on them as fast as they throw it up.—They are striving to pump dry a sinking ship: the water gains on them and they will soon be drowned.—Such is the experience, in every part of the world, of all who think to cleanse themselves from their sins.

I warn every reader of this paper to beware of quack medicines in religion. Beware of supposing that penitence, and reformation, and formality, and priest-craft, can ever give you peace with God. They cannot do it. It is not in them. The man who says they can must be ignorant of two things. He cannot know the length and breadth of human sinfulness: he cannot understand the height and depth of the holiness of God. There never breathed the man or woman on earth who tried to cleanse himself from his sins, and in so doing obtained relief.

If you have found out this truth by experience, be diligent to impart it to others. Show them as plainly as you can their guilt and danger by nature. Tell them, with no less plainness, the immense importance of having their sins forgiven and cleansed away. But then warn them not to waste time in seeking to be cleansed in unlawful fashions. Warn them against the specious advice of 'Mr Legality' and his companions, so vividly described in *Pilgrim's Progress*. Warn them against false remedies and sham medicines for the soul. Send them to the old wicket-gate, described in Scripture, however hard and rough the way may seem. Tell them it is 'the old path and the good way', and that, whatever men may say, it is the only way to obtain cleansing of our sins (Jer. 6:16).

IV. The fourth remark I have to make is this. *The blood of Jesus Christ can cleanse away all our sins.*

I enter on this part of my paper with a thankful heart. I bless God that after setting before my readers the deadly nature of their spiritual disease, I am able to set before them an almighty remedy. But I feel it needful to dwell upon this remedy for a few minutes. A thing of such wondrous efficacy as this 'blood' ought to be clearly understood: there should be no vagueness or mystery in your ideas about it. When you hear of the 'blood of Christ' you ought thoroughly to comprehend what the expression means.

The blood of Christ is that life-blood which the Lord Jesus shed when he died for sinners upon the cross. It is the blood which flowed so freely from his head pierced with thorns, and his hands and feet pierced with nails, and his side pierced with a spear, in the day when he was crucified and slain. The quantity of that blood may very likely have been small; the appearance of that blood was doubtless like that of our own: but never since the day when Adam was first formed out of the dust of the ground, has any blood been shed of such deep importance to the whole family of mankind.

It was blood that had been *long covenanted and promised.* In the day when sin came into the world, God mercifully engaged that 'the Seed of the woman should bruise the serpent's head' (Gen. 3:15). One born of woman should appear one day, and deliver the children of Adam from Satan's power. That Seed of the woman was our Lord Jesus Christ. In the day that he suffered on the cross, he triumphed over Satan and accomplished redemption for mankind. When Jesus shed his life-blood on the cross, the head of the serpent was bruised, and the ancient promise was fulfilled.

It was blood that had been *long typified and prefigured*. Every sacrifice that was offered up by patriarchs, was a testimony of their faith in a greater sacrifice yet to come. Every shedding of the blood of lambs and goats under the Mosaic law was meant to foreshadow the dying of the true Lamb of God for the sin of the world. When Christ was crucified, these sacrifices and types received their full accomplishment. The true sacrifice for sin was at length offered; the real atoning blood was at length shed. From that day the offerings of the Mosaic law were no longer needed. Their work was done. Like old almanacs, they might be laid aside for ever.

It was blood which was of *infinite merit and value* in the sight of God. It was not the blood of one who was nothing more than a singularly holy man, but of one who was God's own 'fellow', very God of very God (Zech. 13:7). It was not the blood of one who died involuntarily, as a martyr for truth, but of one who voluntarily undertook to be the Substitute and Proxy for mankind, to bear their sins and carry their iniquities. It made atonement for man's transgressions; it paid man's enormous debt to God; it provided a way of righteous reconciliation between sinful man and his holy

Maker; it made a road from heaven to earth, by which God could come down to man, and show mercy; it made a road from earth to heaven, by which man could draw near to God, and yet not feel afraid. Without it there could have been no remission of sin. Through it God can be 'just and yet the justifier' of the ungodly (Rom. 3:26). From it a fountain has been formed, wherein sinners can wash and be clean to all eternity.

This wondrous blood of Christ, applied to your conscience, can cleanse you from all sin. It matters nothing what your sins may have been: 'Though they be as scarlet they may be made like snow. Though they be red like crimson they can be made like wool' (Isa. 1:18). From sins of youth and sins of age,—from sins of ignorance and sins of knowledge,—from sins of open profligacy and sins of secret vice,—from sins against law and sins against gospel,—from sins of head, and heart, and tongue, and thought, and imagination,—from sins against each and all of the Ten Commandments,—from all these the blood of Christ can set us free. To this end was it appointed; for this cause was it shed; for this purpose it is still a fountain open to all mankind. That thing which you cannot do for yourself can be done in a moment by this precious fountain. YOU CAN HAVE ALL YOUR SINS CLEANSED AWAY.

In this blood all *the dead saints* have been cleansed hitherto, who are now waiting the resurrection of the just. From Abel, the first of whom we read, down to the last who has fallen asleep today, they have all 'washed their robes, and made them white in the blood of the Lamb' (Rev. 7:14). Not one has entered into rest by his own works and deservings; not one has made himself clean before God by his own goodness and his own strength. They have all 'overcome by the blood of the Lamb' (Rev. 12:11). And their testimony in Paradise is clear and distinct: 'Thou wast slain, and hast redeemed us to God by thy blood, out of every kindred, and tongue, and people, and nation' (Rev. 5:9).

By this blood all *the living saints* of God have peace and hope now. By it they have boldness to enter into the holiest; by it they are justified and made nigh to God; by it their consciences are daily purged and filled with holy confidence. About it all believers are agreed, however much they may differ on other matters. Episcopalians and Presbyterians, Baptists and Methodists,—all are agreed that the blood of Christ is the only thing that can cleanse the soul.—All are agreed that in ourselves we are 'wretched and miserable, and poor, and blind, and naked' (Rev. 3:17). But all are agreed that in the blood of Christ the chief of sinners can be made clean.

Would you like to know what we ministers of the gospel are ordained to do? We are not set apart for no other end than to read services, and administer sacraments, and marry people, and bury the dead. We are not meant to do nothing more than show you the church, or ourselves, or our party. We are set for the work of showing men the 'blood of

Christ'; and except we are continually showing it, we are no true ministers of the gospel.

Would you like to know what is our heart's desire and prayer for the souls to whom we minister? We want to bring them to the 'blood of Christ'. We are not content to see our churches filled, and our ordinances well attended, our congregations numerous, and our cause outwardly flourishing. We want to see men and women coming to this great fountain for sin and uncleanness, and washing their souls in it that they may be clean. Here only is rest for the conscience. Here only is peace for the inward man. Here only is a care for spiritual diseases. Here only is the secret of a light and happy heart. No doubt we have within us a fountain of evil and corruption. But, blessed be God, there is another fountain of greater power still,—even the precious blood of the Lamb; and washing daily in that other fountain, we are clean from all sin.

V. The fifth, and last, remark I have to make is this. *Faith is absolutely necessary, and the only thing necessary, in order to give us an interest in the cleansing blood of Christ.*

I ask the special attention of all my readers to this point. A mistake here is often ruinous to a man's soul. It is a great leak at the bottom of your Christianity if you do not clearly see the true way of union between Christ and the soul.— That way is faith.

Church membership and reception of the sacraments are

no proof that you are washed in Christ's blood. Thousands attend a Christian place of worship, and receive the Lord's supper from the hands of Christian ministers, and yet show plainly that they are not cleansed from their sins. Beware of despising means of grace, if you have any desire to be saved. But never, never forget that church membership is not faith.

Faith is the one thing needful in order to give you the benefit of Christ's cleansing blood. He is called a 'propitiation through faith in his blood'.—'He that believeth on him hath everlasting life.'—'By him all that believe are justified from all things.'—'Being justified by faith we have peace with God, through our Lord Jesus Christ' (Rom. 3:25; John 3:36; Acts 13:39; Rom. 5:1). The wisdom of the whole world will never provide a better answer to an anxious inquirer than that which Paul gave to the Philippian jailer: 'Believe on the Lord Jesus Christ, and thou shalt be saved' (Acts 16:31).—'Art thou convinced of sin?' says the gospel. 'Dost thou really see that thou hast many sins, and art deserving of hell? Dost thou renounce all hope of cleansing thyself from thy sins by thine own power? Then thou art just the man for whom the gospel provides comfort. Behold the atoning blood of Christ! Only trust in it, and this day thou shalt be freely pardoned. Only believe, and this very moment thy sins shall be cleansed away.'—It is only 'Believe and have'. It is only 'Believe and be clean'. Let those who will call such doctrine rant and enthusiasm. I am bold to call it by another name. It is the 'glorious gospel' of the grace of God.

I ask you not to misunderstand my meaning in thus speaking of faith. I do not tell you that faith is the *only* mark of the man whose sins are cleansed away. I do not say that the faith which gives a man an interest in Christ's atoning blood, is ever found *alone*. Saving faith is no barren, solitary grace. It is always accompanied by repentance and personal holiness.—But this I say confidently,—that in the matter of giving the soul an interest in Christ, faith is the only thing required. In the matter of *justification before God*, faith, I repeat emphatically, stands entirely alone. Faith is the hand that lays hold on Christ. Faith begins, faith carries on, faith keeps up the claim which the sinner makes on the Saviour. By faith we are justified. By faith we bathe our souls in the great fountain for sin. By faith we go on obtaining fresh supplies of pardoning mercy all through our journey. By faith we live, and by faith we stand.

Nothing whatever beside this faith is required, in order to your complete justification and cleansing from all sin. Let this sink deeply into your mind. Where is the man that desires to enjoy real comfort from the gospel? Seek, I do entreat you, to have clear and simple views of the nature of saving faith. Beware of those dark, and confused, and muddy notions of faith, by which so many distress their souls. Dismiss from your mind the idea that faith is a mere act of the intellect. It is not assent to doctrines or articles; it is not belief of 'Paley's Evidences' or 'Pearson on the Creed'. It is simply the grasp of a contrite heart on the outstretched hand of an Almighty Saviour,—the repose of a weary head on the bosom of an Almighty Friend.—Cast away all idea of work, or merit, or doing, or performing, or paying, or giving, or buying, or labouring, in the act of believing on Christ. Understand that faith is not giving, but taking,—not paying, but receiving,—not buying, but being enriched. Faith is the eye which looks to the brazen serpent, and looking obtains life and health; it is the mouth which drinks down the reviving medicine, and drinking receives strength and vigour for the whole body; it is the hand of the drowning man which lays hold on the rope thrown to him, and laying hold enables him to be drawn up from the deep water safe and sound. This, and nothing more than this, is the true idea of saving faith. This, and this only, is the faith that is required to give you an interest in the blood of Christ. Believe in this way, and your sins are at once cleansed away!

Nothing whatever except this faith will ever give you an interest in Christ's atoning blood. You may go daily to Christ's church; you may often use Christ's name; you may bow the head at the name of Jesus; you may eat of the bread and wine which Christ commanded to be received. But all this time, without faith, you have neither part nor lot in Christ: without faith, so far as you are concerned, Christ's blood has been shed in vain.

I desire to enter my solemn protest against the modern notions which prevail on this solemn subject. I protest against the opinion which many now maintain, that any are saved by Christ excepting those who believe. There is much vague talk in some quarters about the 'Fatherhood of God' and the 'love of God', as if we who are called 'Evangelical' denied these glorious truths. We do not deny them at all: we hold them as strongly as any. We give place to no man in this matter. But we utterly deny that God is the spiritual Father of any excepting those who are his *children by faith* in Christ Jesus (Gal. 3:26). We utterly deny that men have a right to take comfort in God's love, except they *believe* on him through whom that love has been manifested, even his dear Son. The atoning blood of the Son of God is the grand exhibition of God's love towards sinners. The sinner who desires to be saved, must have personal dealings with him who shed that blood. By personal faith he must wash in it; by personal faith he must drink of it; by personal faith he must put in his own claim to all its blessings. Without this faith there can be no salvation.

Would you know one main object which we ministers have in view in our preaching? We preach that you may *believe.* Faith is the thing that we desire to see produced in your souls; faith is the thing that, once produced, we desire to see growing. We rejoice to see you coming regularly to hear the gospel; we rejoice to see an orderly, well-behaved congregation of worshippers: but faith, faith, faith,—is the grand result which we long to see in your souls. Without faith we cannot feel comfortable about you; without faith you are in imminent danger of hell. According to your faith will be the strength of your Christianity; according to the degree of your faith will be the increase of your peace and hope, and the closeness of your walk with God. You will not wonder that there is nothing we care for so much as your believing.

I hasten to bring my remarks to a conclusion. I have tried to show you five things, and have endeavoured to set them before you in plain language. (1) I have told you that you have many sins. (2) I have told you that it is of the utmost importance to have these sins cleansed away. (3) I have told you that you cannot cleanse away your own sins. (4) I have told you that the blood of Christ cleanseth from all sin. (5) I have told you that faith only is needful, but absolutely needful, to give you any interest in Christ's blood. I have told you what I am firmly persuaded is God's own truth,— the truth on which I desire myself to live and die. I pray God that the Holy Ghost may apply this truth with mighty power to many souls.

Let me wind up all this subject by three words of parting application. Our years are passing quickly away. The night cometh, when no man can work. Yet a little time, and our place in another world will be settled to all eternity. A few more years, and we shall be either in heaven or in hell. Surely this fact alone ought to set us thinking.

1. My first word of application shall be a *question*. I address it to all into whose hands this paper may fall, with-

out distinction or exception. It is a question which concerns deeply every man, woman, and child in the world, whatever be their rank or station. It is the question which rises naturally out of our subject: *'Where are your sins?'*

Remember, I do not ask you what you call yourself in religion. I do not ask you where you go,—or whom you hear,—or to what party you belong—or what are your peculiar opinions about Church or Dissent. I leave such matters alone. I am weary to see the enormous waste of time of which multitudes are yearly guilty in respect to these matters. I am for the realities and substance of Christianity; I want to fix your attention on the things which will look important in the hour of death and at the last day. And say boldly, that one of the first questions which demand your notice, is the question, *'Where are your sins?'*

I am not asking what you intend, or mean, or hope, or resolve to aim at, at some future time; I leave all that to children and fools. Tomorrow is the devil's day, but today is God's. And here, as in God's sight, this very day, while you are reading my paper, I ask you to find in answer to my question: *'Where are your sins?'*

I ask you to mark what I am going to say. I say it calmly, deliberately, advisedly, and with consideration. I tell you that at this moment there are only two places in which your sins can be, and I defy the wisdom of the world to find out a third. Either your sins are UPON YOURSELF, unpardoned, unforgiven, uncleansed, unwashed away,—sinking you daily nearer to hell! Or else your sins are UPON CHRIST, taken away, forgiven, pardoned, blotted out and cleansed away by Christ's precious blood! I am utterly unable to see any third place in which a man's sins can possibly be. I am utterly unable to discover any third alternative. Forgiven or unforgiven,—pardoned or not pardoned,—cleansed away or not cleansed,—this, according to the Bible, is the exact position of everyone's sins. How is it with you? *'Where are your sins?'*

I beseech you to lay this question to heart, and never to rest till you can give it an answer. I do entreat you to examine your own state to prove your own spiritual condition,—and to find out how matters stand between yourself and God. Let the time past suffice for trifling and indecision about your soul. Give it up,—give it up,—give it up for ever. Let the time past suffice for a mere formal, aimless, meaningless, comfortless religion. Lay it aside, lay it aside,—lay it aside for ever. Be real; be thorough; be in earnest. Deal with your soul as a reasonable being; deal with it as one who feels that eternal interests are at stake; deal with it as one who has made up his mind, and is determined to live in suspense no longer. Oh, resolve this very day to find an answer to my question: *'Where are your sins?' Are they on yourself? or are they on Christ?*

2. My second word of application shall be an *invitation*. I address it to all who feel unable to give a satisfactory answer to the question of my paper. I address it to all who feel

sinful, and lost, and condemned, and unfit to die. It is that invitation which is the glory of the gospel. I say to you, *'Come to Christ, and be cleansed in his blood without delay.'*

I know not what you may have been in your past life: it matters nothing. You may have broken every commandment under heaven; you may have sinned with a high hand against light and knowledge; you may have despised a father's warnings and a mother's tears; you may have run greedily into every excess of riot, and plunged into every kind of abominable profligacy: you may have turned your back entirely on God, his day, his house, his ministers, his Word. I say again it matters nothing.—Do you feel your sins? Are you sick of them? Are you ashamed of them? Are you weary of them? Then *come to Christ* just as you are, and Christ's blood shall make you clean.

I see you lingering and doubting, and fancying the news too good to be true. I hear the devil whispering in your ear, 'You are too bad; you are too wicked to be saved.' I charge you, in God's name, not to give way to such doubts. I remind you that Satan always was a liar. One time he told you it was 'too soon' for religion: and now he tells you it is 'too late'. I tell you confidently, that Jesus Christ is 'able to save to the uttermost all who come to God by him' (Heb. 7:25). I tell you confidently, that he has received, cleansed, and pardoned thousands as bad as you. He never changes. Only come to him, and his blood shall cleanse you from all sin.

33

I can well fancy that you feel at a loss, and know not what to do. I can well believe that you do not see which way to turn, or what step to take, or in what manner to follow out my counsel. *I bid you go and say so to the Lord Jesus Christ!* I bid you seek some quiet solitary place, and pour out your heart before him. Tell him that you are a poor miserable sinner. Tell him that you know not how to pray, or what to say, or what to do. But tell him that you have heard something about his blood cleansing a man from all sin, and entreat him to think on you, and cleanse your soul. Oh, take this advice and who can tell but you may say one day, 'The blood of Christ does indeed cleanse a man from all sin.'

For the last time I offer my invitation. I stand in the life-boat alongside the wreck to which you are clinging, and I entreat you to come in. The day is far spent; the night is coming on; the clouds are gathering; the waves are rising. Yet a little time and the old wreck of this world will go to pieces. Come into the life-boat; come in and be safe. Come to the blood of Christ; wash, and be clean. Come with all your sins to Christ, and cast them on him. He will bear them away; he will cleanse them; he will pardon them. Only believe and be saved.

3. My last word shall be *an exhortation*. I address it to all who have been taught by the Spirit to feel their sins, and have fled to the hope set before them in the gospel. I address it to all who have discovered the grand truth that they are

guilty sinners, and have washed in the blood of Christ in order to have their sins cleansed away. That exhortation shall be short and simple. I bid them 'cling to Christ'.

Cling to Christ, I say: and never forget your debt to him. Sinners you were, when you were first called by the Holy Ghost, and fled to Jesus. Sinners you have been, even at your best, from the day of your conversion. Sinners you will find yourselves to your dying hour, having nothing to boast of in yourselves. Then cling to Christ.

Cling to Christ, I say: and make use of his atoning blood every day. Go to him every morning, as your morning sacrifice, and confess your need of his salvation. Go to him every night, after the bustle of the day, and plead for fresh absolution. Wash in the great fountain every evening, after all the defilement of contact with the world. 'He that is washed, needeth not save to wash his feet.' But his feet he needs to wash (John 13:10).

Cling to Christ, I say: and show the world how you love him. Show it by obedience to his commandments. Show it by conformity to his image. Show it by following his example. Make your Master's cause lovely and beautiful before men, by your own holiness of temper and conversation. Let all the world see that he who is much forgiven is the man who loves much, and that he who loves most is the man who does most for Christ (Luke 7:47).

Cling to Christ, I say: and have high thoughts of the atonement made by his blood upon the cross. Think highly of his incarnation and his example,—think highly of his miracles and his words,—think highly of his resurrection, and intercession, and coming again. But think highest of all of Christ's sacrifice, and the propitiation made by his death. Contend earnestly for the old faith concerning his atonement. See in the old doctrine that he died as a Substitute for sinners, the only solution of a thousand passages in the Old Testament, and a hundred passages in the New. Never, never be ashamed to let men know that you derive all your comfort from the atoning blood of Christ, and from his substitution for you on the cross.

Cling to Christ, I say lastly: and make much of the old foundation truths concerning salvation by his blood. These are the old friends to which our souls will turn at last in the hour of our departure. These are the ancient doctrines on which we shall lean back our aching heads, when life is ebbing away and death is in sight. We shall not ask ourselves then whether we have been Episcopalians or Presbyterians, Churchmen or Dissenters. We shall not find comfort then in new-fangled notions and human invention,—in baptism and church membership,—in sects and parties,—in ceremonies and forms. Nothing will do us good then but the blood of Christ. Nothing will support us then but the witness of the Spirit, that in the blood of Jesus we have washed, and by that blood have been made clean.

I commend these things to the serious attention of all who read this volume. If you never knew these things before, may you soon become acquainted with them! If you have known them in time past, may you know them better for time to come! We can never know too well the right answer to the mighty question,—*'Where are your sins?'*

2

Few Saved?

Are there few that be saved?—Luke 13:23.

I TAKE it for granted that every reader of this paper calls himself a Christian. You would not like to be reckoned a Deist, or an infidel. You profess to believe the Bible to be true. The birth of Christ the Saviour,—the death of Christ the Saviour,—the salvation provided by Christ the Saviour,—all these are facts which you have probably never doubted. But, after all, will Christianity like this profit you anything at last? Will it do your soul any good when you die? In one word,—*Shall you be saved?*

It may be you are now young, healthy and strong. Perhaps you never had a day's illness in your life, and scarcely know what it is to feel weakness and pain. You scheme and plan for future years, and feel as if death was far away, and out of sight. Yet, remember, death sometimes cuts off young people in the flower of their days. The strong and healthy of the family do not always live the longest. Your sun may go down before your life has reached its mid-day. Yet a little

39

while, and you may be lying in a narrow, silent home, and the daisies may be growing over your grave. And then, consider—*Shall you be saved?*

It may be you are rich and prosperous in this world. You have money, and all that money can command. You have 'honour, love, obedience, troops of friends'. But, remember, 'riches are not for ever'. You cannot keep them longer than a few years. 'It is appointed unto men once to die, and after this the judgment' (Prov. 27:24; Heb. 9:27). And then, consider,—*Shall you be saved?*

It may be you are poor and needy. You have scarcely enough to provide food and raiment for yourself and family. You are often distressed for want of comforts, which you have no power to get. Like Lazarus, you seem to have 'evil things' only, and not good. But, nevertheless, you take comfort in the thought that there will be an end of all this. There is a world to come, where poverty and want shall be unknown. Yet, consider a moment,—*Shall you be saved?*

It may be you have a weak and sickly body. You hardly know what it is to be free from pain. You have so long parted company with health, that you have almost forgotten what it is like. You have often said in the morning, 'Would God it were evening'—and in the evening, 'Would God it were morning.' There are days when you are tempted by very weariness to cry out with Jonah, 'It is better for me to die than to live' (Jon. 4:3). But, remember, death is not all. There is something else beyond the grave. And then, consider,—*Shall you be saved?*

If it was an easy thing to be saved, I would not write as I do in this volume. But is it so? Let us see.

If the common opinion of the world as to the number of the saved was correct, I would not trouble men with searching and hard questions. But is it so? Let us see.

If God had never spoken plainly in the Bible about the number of the saved, I might well be silent. But is it so? Let us see.

If experience and facts left it doubtful whether many or few would be saved, I might hold my peace. But is it so? Let us see.

There are four points which I propose to examine in considering the subject before us.

I. Let me explain *what it is to be saved.*

II. Let me point out *the mistakes which are common in the world about the number of the saved.*

III. Let me show what *the Bible says about the number of the saved.*

IV. Let me bring forward some *plain facts as to the number of the saved.*

A calm examination of these four points, in a day of wide-spread carelessness about vital religion, will be found of vast importance to our souls.

I. *First of all, let me explain what it is to be saved.*

This is a matter that must be cleared up. Till we know this, we shall make no progress. By being 'saved' I may mean one thing, and you may mean another. Let me show you what the Bible says it is to be 'saved', and then there will be no misunderstanding.

To be saved, is not merely to profess and call ourselves Christians. We may have all the outward parts of Christianity, and yet be lost after all. We may be baptized into Christ's church,—go to Christ's table,—have Christian knowledge,—be reckoned Christian men and women— and yet be dead souls all our lives,—and at last, in the judgment day, be found on Christ's left hand, among the goats. No: this is not salvation! Salvation is something far higher and deeper than this. Now what is it?

(*a*) To be saved, is to be delivered in this present life from the *guilt of sin*, by faith in Jesus Christ, the Saviour. It is to be pardoned, justified, and freed from every charge of sin, by faith in Christ's blood and mediation. Whosoever with his heart believes on the Lord Jesus Christ, is a saved soul. He shall not perish. He shall have eternal life. This is the first part of salvation, and the root of all the rest. But this is not all.

(*b*) To be saved, is to be delivered in this present life from *the power of sin*, by being born again, and sanctified by Christ's spirit. It is to be freed from the hateful dominion of sin, the world, and the devil, by having a new nature put in us by the Holy Ghost. Whosoever is thus renewed in the spirit of his mind, and converted, is a saved soul. He shall not perish. He shall enter into the glorious kingdom of God. This is the second part of salvation. But this is not all.

(*c*) To be saved, is to be delivered in the day of judgment, from all *the awful consequences of sin*. It is to be declared blameless, spotless, faultless, and complete in Christ, while others are found guilty, and condemned for ever. It is to hear those comfortable words 'Come, ye blessed!' while others are hearing those fearful words, 'Depart, ye cursed!' (Matt. 25:34, 41). It is to be owned and confessed by Christ, as one of his dear children and servants, while others are disowned and cast off for ever. It is to be pronounced free from the portion of the wicked,—the worm that never dies,—the fire that is not quenched,—the weeping, wailing and gnashing of teeth, that never ends. It is to receive the reward prepared for the righteous, in the day of Christ's second coming;—the glorious body,—the kingdom that is incorruptible,—the crown that fadeth not away,—and the joy that is for evermore. This is *complete salvation*. This is the 'redemption' for which true Christians are bid to look and long (Luke 21:28). This is the heritage of all men and women who believe and are born again. By faith they are saved already. In the eye of God their final salvation is an absolutely certain thing. Their names are in the Book of Life. Their mansions in heaven are even now prepared. But still there is a fulness of redemption and salvation which they do not attain to while they are in the body. They are saved from the guilt and power of sin;—but not from the necessity of watching and praying against it. They are saved from the fear and love of the world;—but not from the necessity of daily fighting with it. They are saved from the service of the devil;—but they are not saved from being vexed by his temptations. But when Christ comes the salvation of believers shall be complete. They possess it already in the bud. They shall see it then in the flower.

Such is salvation. It is to be saved from the guilt, power, and consequences of sin. It is to believe and be sanctified now, and to be delivered from the wrath of God in the last day. He that has the first part in the life that now is, shall undoubtedly have the second part in the life to come. Both parts of it hang together. What God has joined together, let no man dare to put asunder. Let none dream he shall ever be saved at last, if he is not born again first. Let none doubt, if he is born again here, that he shall assuredly be saved hereafter.

Let it never be forgotten that the chief object of a minister of the gospel is to set forward *the salvation of souls*. I lay it down as a certain fact that he is no true minister who does not feel this. Talk not of a man's orders! All may have been done correctly, and according to rule. He may wear a black coat, and be called a 'reverend' man. But if the saving of souls is not the grand interest—the ruling passion—the absorbing thought of his heart,—he is no true minister of the gospel: he is a hireling, and not a shepherd. Congregations may have called him,—but he is not called by the Holy Ghost. Bishops may have ordained him,—but not Christ.

For what purpose do men suppose that ministers are sent forth? Is it merely to wear a surplice,—and read the services,—and preach a certain number of sermons? Is it merely to administer the sacraments, and officiate at weddings and funerals? Is it merely to get a comfortable living, and be in a respectable profession? No, indeed! we are sent forth for other ends than these. We are sent to turn men from darkness to light, and from the power of Satan unto God. We are sent to persuade men to flee from the wrath to come. We are sent to draw men from the service of the world to the service of God,—to awaken the sleeping;—to arouse the careless,—and 'by all means to save some' (1 Cor. 9:22).

Think not that all is done when we have set up regular services, and persuaded people to attend them. Think not that all is done, when full congregations are gathered, and the Lord's table is crowded, and the parish school is filled. We want to see manifest work of the Spirit among people,—an evident sense of sin,—a lively faith in Christ,—a decided change of heart,—a distinct separation from the world,—a holy walk with God. In one word, *we want to see souls saved*; and we are fools and impostors,—blind leaders of the blind,—if we rest satisfied with anything less.

After all the grand object of having a religion is *to be saved*. This is the great question that we have to settle with our consciences. The matter for our consideration is not whether we go to church or chapel,—whether we go through certain forms and ceremonies,—whether we observe certain days, and perform a certain number of religious duties. The matter is whether, after all, we shall be 'saved'. Without this all our religious doings are weariness and labour in vain.

Never, never let us be content with anything short of a saving religion. Surely to be satisfied with a religion which neither gives peace in life, nor hope in death, nor glory in the world to come, is childish folly.

II. Let me, in the second place, *point out the mistakes which are common in the world about the number of the saved.*

I need not go far for evidence on this subject. I will speak of things which every man may see with his own eyes, and hear with his own ears.

I will try to show that there is a wide-spread delusion abroad about this matter, and that this very delusion is one of the greatest dangers to which our souls are exposed.

(*a*) What then do men generally think about the spiritual state of others while *they are alive*? What do they think of the souls of their relations, and friends, and neighbours, and acquaintances? Let us just see how that question can be answered.

They know that all around them are going to die, and to be judged. They know that they have souls to be lost or saved. And what, to all appearance, do they consider their end is likely to be?

Do they think those around them are in danger of hell? There is nothing whatever to show they think so. They eat and drink together; they laugh, and talk, and walk, and work together. They seldom or never speak to one another of God and eternity,—of heaven and of hell. I ask anyone, who knows the world, as in the sight of God, is it not so?

Will they allow that anybody is wicked or ungodly? Never, hardly, whatever may be his way of life. He may be a breaker of the Sabbath; he may be a neglecter of the Bible; he may be utterly without evidence of true religion. No matter! His friends will often tell you, that he may not make so much profession as some, but that he has a 'good heart' at the bottom, and is not a wicked man. I ask anyone, who knows the world, as in God's sight, is it not so?

And what does all this prove? It proves that men flatter themselves there is no great difficulty in getting to heaven. It proves plainly that men are of opinion that most persons will be saved.

(*b*) But what do men generally think about this spiritual state of others *after they are dead*? Let us just see how this question can be answered.

Men allow, if they are not infidels, that all who die have gone to a place of happiness, or of misery. And to which of these two places do they seem to think the greater part of persons go, when they leave this world?

I say, without fear of contradiction, that there is an unhappily common fashion of speaking well of the condition of all who have departed this life. It matters little, apparently, how a man has behaved while he lived. He may have given no signs of repentance, or faith in Christ; he may have been ignorant of the plan of salvation set forth in the gospel; he may have shown no evidence whatever of conversion or sanctification; he may have lived and died like a creature without a soul. And yet, as soon as this man is dead, people will dare to say that he is 'probably happier than ever he was in his life'. They will tell you complacently, they 'hope he is gone to a better world'. They will shake their heads gravely, and say they 'hope he is in heaven'. They will follow him to the grave without fear and trembling, and speak of his death afterwards as 'a blessed change for him'. They may have disliked him, and thought him a bad man while he was alive; but the moment he is dead they turn round in their opinions and say they trust he is gone to heaven! I have no wish to hurt anyone's feelings. I only ask anyone, who knows the world,—Is it not true?

And what does it all prove? It just supplies one more awful proof that men are determined to believe it is an easy business to get to heaven. Men will have it that most persons are saved.

(c) But again, what do men generally *think of ministers*

who preach fully the doctrines of the New Testament? Let us see how this question can be answered.

Send a clergyman into a parish who shall 'declare all the counsel of God', and 'keep back nothing that is profitable'. Let him be one who shall clearly proclaim justification by faith,—regeneration by the Spirit,—and holiness of life. Let him be one who shall draw the line distinctly between the converted and the unconverted, and give both to sinners and to saints their portion. Let him frequently produce out of the New Testament a plain, unanswerable description of the true Christian's character. Let him show that no man who does not possess that character can have any reasonable hope of being saved. Let him constantly press that description on the consciences of his hearers, and urge upon them repeatedly that every soul who dies without that character will be lost. Let him do this, ably and affectionately, and after all, what will the result be?

The result will be, that while some few repent and are saved, the great majority of his hearers will not receive and believe his doctrine. They may not oppose him publicly. They may even esteem him, and respect him as an earnest, sincere, kind-hearted man, who means well. But they will go no further. He may show them the express words of Christ and his apostles; he may quote text upon text, and passage upon passage: it will be to no purpose. The great majority of his hearers will think him 'too strict', and 'too close', and 'too particular'. They will say among themselves, that the

49

world is not so bad as the minister seems to think,—and that people cannot be so good as the minister wants them to be,—and that after all, they hope they shall be all right at the last! I appeal to any minister of the gospel, who has been any length of time in the ministry, whether I am not stating the truth. Are not these things so?

And what does it prove? It just makes one more proof that men generally are resolved to think that salvation is not a very hard business, and that after all most people will be saved.

Now what solid reason can men show us for these common opinions? Upon what Scripture do they build this notion, that salvation is an easy business, and that most people will be saved? What revelation of God can they show us, to satisfy us that these opinions are sound and true?

They have none,—literally none at all. They have not a text of Scripture which, fairly interpreted, supports their views. They have not a reason which will bear examination. They speak smooth things about one another's spiritual state, just because they do not like to allow there is danger. They build up one another into an easy, self-satisfied state of soul, in order to soothe their consciences and make things pleasant. They cry 'Peace, peace,' over one another's graves, because they want it to be so, and would fain persuade themselves that so it is. Surely against such hollow, foundationless opinions as these, a minister of the gospel may well protest.

The plain truth is that the world's opinion is worth nothing in matters of religion. About the price of an ox, or a horse, or a farm, or the value of labour,—about wages and work,—about money, cotton, coals, iron and corn,—about arts, and sciences, and manufactures,—about railways, and commerce, and trade, and politics,—about all such things the men of the world may give a correct opinion. But we must beware, if we love life, of being guided by man's judgment in the things that concern salvation. 'The natural man receiveth not the things of the Spirit of God, for they are foolishness unto him' (1 Cor. 2:14).

Let us remember, above all, that it never will do to think as others do, if we want to get to heaven. No doubt it is easy work to 'go with the crowd' in religious matters. It will save us much trouble to swim with the stream and tide. We shall be spared much ridicule: we shall be freed from much unpleasantness. But let us remember, once for all, that the world's mistakes about salvation are many and dangerous. Unless we are on our guard against them we shall never be saved.

III. Let me show, in the third place, *what the Bible says about the number of the saved.*

There is only one standard of truth and error to which we ought to appeal. That standard is the Holy Scripture. Whatsoever is there written we must receive and believe: whatsoever cannot be proved by Scripture we ought to refuse.

Can any reader of this paper subscribe to this? If he

cannot, there is little chance of his being moved by any words of mine. If he can, let him give me his attention for a few moments, and I will tell him some solemn things.

Let us look, then, for one thing, at one single text of Scripture, and examine it well. We shall find it in Matthew 7:13, 14:—'Enter ye in at the strait gate: for wide is the gate, and broad is the way that leadeth to destruction, and many there be which go in thereat: because strait is the gate, and narrow is the way which leadeth unto life, and *few there be that find it.*' Now these are the words of our Lord Jesus Christ. They are the words of him who was very God, and whose words shall never pass away. They are the words of him who knew what was in man,—who knew things to come, and things past,—who knew that he should judge all men at the last day. And what do those words mean? Are they words which no man can understand without a knowledge of Hebrew or Greek? No: they are not! Are they a dark, unfulfilled prophecy, like the visions in Revelation, or the description of Ezekiel's temple? No: they are not! Are they a deep mysterious saying, which no human intellect can fathom? No: they are not! The words are clear, plain, and unmistakable. Ask any labouring man who can read, and he will tell you so. There is only one meaning which can be attached to them. Their meaning is, that many people will be lost, and few will be found saved.

Let us look, in the next place, at the whole history of mankind as respects religion, as we have it given in the

Bible. Let us go through the whole four thousand years, over which the history of the Bible reaches. Let us find, if we can, one single period of time at which godly people were many, and ungodly peoples were few.

How was it in the *days of Noah*? The earth we are told expressly was 'filled with violence'. The imagination of man's heart was only 'evil continually' (Gen. 6:5, 12). 'All flesh had corrupted his way.' The loss of Paradise was forgotten. The warnings of God, by Noah's mouth, were despised. And at length, when the flood came on the world and drowned every living thing, there were but eight people who had faith enough to flee for refuge to the ark! And were there many saved in those days? Let any honest reader of the Bible give an answer to that question. There can be no doubt what the answer must be.

How was it in the *days of Abraham, and Isaac, and Lot*? It is evident that in the matter of religion they stood very much alone. The family from which they were taken was a family of idolaters. The nations among whom they lived were sunk in gross darkness and sin. When Sodom and Gomorrah were burned there were not five righteous people to be found in the four cities of the plain. When Abraham and Isaac desired to find wives for their sons, there was not a woman in the land where they sojourned to whom they could wish to see them married. And were there many saved in those days? Let any honest reader of the Bible give an answer to that question. There can be no doubt what the answer must be.

How was it with Israel in the *days of the judges*? No one can read the book of Judges, and not be struck with the sad examples of man's corruption which it affords. Time after time we are told of the people forsaking God, and following idols. In spite of the plainest warnings, they joined affinity with the Canaanites, and learned their works. Time after time we read of their being oppressed by foreign kings, because of their sins, and then miraculously delivered. Time after time we read of the deliverance being forgotten, and of the people returning to their former sins, like the sow that is washed to her wallowing in the mire. And were there many saved in those days? Let any honest reader of the Bible give an answer to that question. There can be no doubt what the answer must be.

How was it with Israel in the *days of the kings*? From Saul, the first king, down to Zedekiah, the last king, their history is a melancholy account of backsliding, and declension, and idolatry,—with a few bright exceptional periods. Even under the best kings there seems to have been a vast amount of unbelief and ungodliness, which only lay hid for a season, and burst out at the first favourable opportunity. Over and over again we find that under the most zealous kings 'the high places were not taken away'. Mark how even David speaks of the state of things around him: 'Help, Lord, for the godly man ceaseth; for the faithful fail from among the children of men' (Psa. 12:1). Mark how Isaiah describes the condition of Judah and Jerusalem: 'The whole head is sick, and the whole heart faint. From the sole of the foot, even unto the crown of the head, there is no soundness in it.'—'Except the Lord of hosts had left unto us a very small remnant, we should have been as Sodom, and should have been like unto Gomorrah' (Isa. 1:5-9). Mark how Jeremiah describes his time: 'Run ye to and fro through the streets of Jerusalem, and see now, and know, and seek in the broad places thereof, if ye can find a man, if there be any that executeth judgment, that seeketh the truth, and I will pardon it' (Jer. 5:1). Mark how Ezekiel speaks of the men of his times: 'The word of the Lord came unto me, saying, Son of man, the house of Israel is to me become dross: all they are brass, and iron, and tin and lead in the midst of the furnace: they are even the dross of silver' (Ezek. 22:17, 18). Mark what he says in the sixteenth and twenty-third chapters of his prophecy about the kingdoms of Judah, and Israel. And were there many saved in those days? Let any honest reader of the Bible give an answer to that question. There can be no doubt what the answer must be.

How was it with the Jews *when our Lord Jesus Christ was on earth*? The words of St John are the best account of their spiritual state: 'He came unto his own, and his own received him not' (John 1:11). He lived as no one born of woman had ever lived before,—a blameless, harmless, holy life. 'He went about doing good' (Acts 10:38). He preached as no one ever preached before. Even the officers of his enemies confessed, 'Never man spake like this man' (John 7:46). He did miracles to confirm his ministry, which, at first sight, we might have fancied would have convinced the most hardened. But, notwithstanding all this, the vast majority of the Jews refused to believe him. Follow our Lord in all his travels over Palestine, and you will always find the same story. Follow him into the city, and follow him into the wilderness; follow him to Capernaum and Nazareth, and follow him to Jerusalem; follow him among Scribes and Pharisees, and follow him among Sadducees and Herodians: everywhere you will arrive at the same result. They were amazed;—they were silenced;—they were astonished;—they wondered;—but very few became disciples! The immense proportion of the nation would have none of his doctrine, and crowned all their wickedness by putting him to death. And were there many saved in those days? Let any honest reader of the Bible give an answer to that question. There can be no doubt what the answer must be.

How was it with the world in the *days of the apostles*? If ever there was a period when true religion flourished it was then. Never did the Holy Ghost call into the fold of Christ so many souls in the same space of time. Never were there so many conversions under the preaching of the gospel as when Paul and his fellow-labourers were the preachers. But still, it is plain from the Acts of the Apostles, that true Christianity was 'everywhere spoken against' (Acts 28:22). It is evident that in every city, even in Jerusalem itself, true Christians were a small minority.

We read of perils of all kinds which the apostles had to go through,—not only perils from without, but perils from within,—not only perils from the heathen, but perils from false brethren. We hardly read of a single city visited by Paul where he was not in danger from open violence and persecution. We see plainly, by some of his epistles, that the professing churches were mixed bodies, in which there were many rotten members. We find him telling the Philippians a painful part of his experience,—'Many walk, of whom I tell you, even weeping, that they are the enemies of the cross of Christ, whose end is destruction, whose god is their belly, and whose glory is their shame, who mind earthly things' (Phil. 3:18, 19). And were there many saved in those days? Let any honest reader of the Bible give an answer to this question. There can be no doubt what that answer must be.

I ask any honest-minded unprejudiced reader of the volume to weigh well the lessons of the Bible which I have just brought forward. Surely they are weighty and solemn, and deserve serious attention.

Let no one think to evade their force by saying that the Bible only tells the story of the Jews. Think not to comfort yourself by saying that 'perhaps the Jews were more wicked than other nations, and many people were probably saved among other nations, though few were saved among the Jews'. You forget that this argument tells against you. You forget that the Jews had light and privileges which the

Gentiles had not, and with all their sins and faults, were probably the holiest and most moral nation upon earth. As to the moral state of people among the Assyrians, and Egyptians, and Greeks, and Romans, it is fearful to think what it must have been. But this we may be sure of,—that if many were ungodly among the Jews, the number was far greater among the Gentiles. If few were saved in the green tree, alas, how much fewer must have been saved in the dry!

The sum of the whole matter is this: the Bible and the men of the world speak very differently about the number of the saved. According to the Bible, few will be saved: according to the men of the world, many.—According to the men of the world few are going to hell: according to the Bible few are going to heaven.—According to the men of the world salvation is an easy business: according to the Bible the way is narrow and the gate is strait.—According to the men of the world few will be found at last seeking admission into heaven when too late: according to the Bible many will be in that sad condition, and will cry in vain, 'Lord, Lord, open to us.' Yet the Bible was never wrong yet. The most unlikely and improbable prophecies about Tyre, Egypt, Babylon, and Nineveh, have all come true to the letter. And as in other matters, so it will be about the number of the saved. The Bible will prove quite right and the men of the world quite wrong.

IV. Let me show, in the last place, *some plain facts about the number of the saved*.

I ask particular attention to this part of the subject. I know well that people flatter themselves that the world is far better and wiser than it was 1800 years ago. We have churches, and schools, and books. We have civilization, and liberty, and good laws. We have a far higher standard of morality in society than that which once prevailed. We have the power of obtaining comforts and enjoyments which our forefathers knew nothing of. Steam, and gas, and electricity, and chemistry, have effected wonders for us. All this is perfectly true. I see it, and I am thankful. But all this does not diminish the importance of the question.—*Are there few or many of us likely to be saved?*

I am thoroughly satisfied that the importance of this question is painfully overlooked. I am persuaded that the views of most people about the quantity of unbelief and sin in the world, are utterly inadequate and incorrect. I am convinced that very few people, whether ministers or private Christians, at all realize how few there are in a way to be saved. I want to draw attention to the subject, and I will therefore bring forward a few plain facts about it.

But where shall I go for these facts? I might easily turn to the millions of heathen, who in various parts of the world are worshipping they know not what. But I shall not do so.—I might easily turn to the millions of Mahometans who honour the Koran more than the Bible, and the false prophet of Mecca more than Christ. But I shall not do so.—I might easily turn to the millions of Roman Catholics who are making the Word of God of none effect by their traditions. But I shall not do so. I shall look nearer home. I shall draw my facts from the land in which I live, and then ask every honest reader whether it be not strictly true that *few are saved*.

I invite any intelligent reader of these pages to imagine himself in any parish in Protestant England or Scotland at this day. Choose which you please, a town parish, or a country parish,—a great parish or a small. Let us take our New Testaments in our hands. Let us sift the Christianity of the inhabitants of this parish, family by family, and man by man. Let us put on one side anyone who does not possess the New Testament evidence of being a true Christian. Let us deal honestly and fairly in the investigation, and not allow anyone to be a true Christian who does not come up to the New Testament standard of faith and practice. Let us count every man a saved soul in whom we see something of Christ,—some evidence of true repentance,—some evidence of saving faith in Jesus,—some evidence of real Evangelical holiness. Let us reject every man in whom, on the most charitable construction, we cannot see these evidences, as one 'weighed in the balances, and found wanting'. Let us apply this sifting process to any parish in this land, and see what the result would be.

(*a*) Let us set aside, first of all, those persons in a parish who are *living in any kind of open sin*. By these I mean such as fornicators, and adulterers, and liars, and thieves, and drunkards, and cheats, and revilers, and extortioners. About these I think there can be no difference of opinion. The Bible says plainly, that 'they which do such things, shall not inherit the kingdom of God' (Gal. 5:21). Now will these persons be saved? The answer is clear to my own mind: In their present condition they will not.

(*b*) Let us set aside, in the next place, those persons who are *Sabbath-breakers*. I mean by this expression, those who seldom or never go to a place of worship, though they have the power,—those who do not give the Sabbath to God, but to themselves,—those who think of nothing but doing their own ways, and finding their own pleasure upon Sundays. They show plainly that they are not meet for heaven! The inhabitants of heaven would be company they could not like. The employments of heaven would be a weariness to them, and not a joy. Now will these persons be saved? The answer is clear to my mind: In their present condition they will not.

(*c*) Let us set aside, in the next place, all those persons who are *careless and thoughtless Christians*. I mean by this expression, those who attend many of the outward ordinances of religion, but show no signs of taking any real interest in its doctrines and substance. They care little whether the minister preaches the gospel or not. They care little whether they hear a good sermon or not. They would care little if all the Bibles in the world were burned. They would care little if an Act of Parliament were passed forbidding anyone to pray. In short religion is not the 'one thing needful' with them. Their treasure is on earth. They are just like Gallio, to whom it mattered little whether people were Jews or Christians: he 'cared for none of these things' (Acts 18:17). Now will these persons be saved? The answer is clear to my own mind: In their present condition they will not.

(*d*) Let us set aside, in the next place, all those who are *formalists and self-righteous*. I mean by this expression, those who value themselves on their own regularity in the use of the forms of Christianity, and depend either directly or indirectly on their own doings for their acceptance with God. I mean all who rest their souls on any work but the work of Christ, or any righteousness but the righteousness of Christ. Of such the Apostle Paul has expressly testified, 'By the deeds of the law shall no flesh living be justified.'—'Other foundation can no man lay than that is laid, which is Jesus Christ' (Rom. 3:20; 1 Cor. 3:11). And dare we say, in the face of such texts, that such as these will be saved? The answer is plain to my own mind: In their present condition they will not.

(*e*) Let us set aside, in the next place, all those who *know the gospel with their heads, but do not obey it with their hearts*. These are those unhappy persons who have eyes to see the way of life, but have not will or courage to walk in it. They approve sound doctrine. They will not listen to preaching which does not contain it. But the fear of man, or the cares of the world, or the love of money, or the dread of offending relations, perpetually holds them back. They will not come out boldly, and take up the cross, and confess Christ before men. Of these also the Bible speaks expressly: 'Faith, if it hath not works, is dead, being alone.'—'To him that knoweth to do good, and doeth it not, to him it is sin.'—'If any man is ashamed of me and of my words, of him will the Son of man be ashamed when he shall come in his own glory, and in his Father's, and of the holy angels' (James 2:17; 4:17; Luke 9:26). Shall we say that such as these will be saved? The answer is clear to my own mind: In their present condition they will not.

(*f*) Let us set aside, in the last place, all those who are *hypocritical professors*. I mean by that expression, all those whose religion consists in talk and high profession, and in nothing besides. These are they of whom the prophet Ezekiel speaks, saying, 'With their mouth they show much love, but their heart goeth after their covetousness.'—'They profess that they know God, but in works they deny him.'— They 'have a form of godliness, but they have not the power' of it (Ezek. 33:31; Titus 1:16; 2 Tim. 3:5). They are saints at church, and saints to talk to in public. But they are not saints in private, and in their own homes; and worst of all, they are not saints in heart. There can be no dispute about such persons. Shall we say that they will be saved? There can only be one answer: In their present condition they will not.

And now, after setting aside these classes which I have described, I ask any sensible thinking reader to tell me how many persons in any parish in England will there be left behind? How many after sifting a parish thoroughly and honestly,—how many men and women will remain who are in a way to be saved? How many true penitents,—how many real believers in Christ,—how many truly holy people will there be found? I put it to the conscience of every reader of this volume to give an honest answer, as in the sight of God. I ask you whether, after sifting a parish with the Bible in the fashion described, you can come to any conclusion but this,—that few persons,—sadly few persons, are in a way to be saved!

It is a painful conclusion to arrive at, but I know not how it can be avoided. It is a fearful and tremendous thought, that there should be so many Churchmen in England, and so many Dissenters, so many seat-holders, and so many pew-renters, so many hearers, and so many communicants,—and yet, after all, so few in a way to be saved! But the only question is, Is it not true?—It is vain to shut our eyes against facts. It is useless to pretend not to see what is going on around us. The statements of the Bible and the facts of the world we live in will lead us to the same conclusion: *Many are being lost, and few being saved!*

(*a*) I know well that many do not believe what I am saying, because *they think there is an immense quantity of deathbed repentance.* They flatter themselves that multitudes who do not live religious lives will yet die religious deaths. They take comfort in the thought that vast numbers of persons turn to God in their last illness and are saved at the eleventh hour. I will only remind such persons that all the experience of ministers is utterly against the theory. People generally die just as they have lived. True repentance is never too late:—but repentance deferred to the last hours of life is seldom true. A man's life is the surest evidence of his spiritual state, and if lives are to be witnesses, then few are likely to be saved.

(*b*) I know well that many do not believe what I am saying, because *they fancy it contradicts the mercy of God*. They dwell on the love to sinners which the gospel reveals. They point to the offers of pardon and forgiveness which abound in the Bible. They ask us if we maintain, in the face of all this, that only few people will be saved. I answer, I will go as far as anyone in exalting God's mercy in Christ, but I cannot shut my eyes against the fact that this mercy profits no man so long as it is wilfully refused. I see nothing wanting, on God's part, for man's salvation. I see room in heaven for the chief of sinners. I see willingness in Christ to receive the most ungodly. I see power in the Holy Ghost to renew the most ungodly. But I see, on the other hand, desperate unbelief in man: he will not believe what God tells him in the Bible. I see desperate pride in man: he will not bow his heart to receive the gospel as a little child. I see desperate sloth in man: he will not take the trouble to arise and call upon God. I see desperate worldliness in man: he will not loose his hold on the poor perishable things of time, and consider eternity. In short, I see the words of our Lord continually verified: 'Ye will not come unto me that ye might have life' (John 5:40), and therefore I am driven to the sorrowful conclusion that few are likely to be saved.

(c) I know well that many will not believe what I am saying, because *they refuse to observe the evil there is in the world*. They live in the midst of a little circle of good people: they know little of anything that goes on in the world outside that circle. They tell us the world is a world which is rapidly improving and going on to perfection. They count up on their fingers the number of good ministers whom they have heard and seen in the last year. They call our attention to the number of religious societies, and religious meetings, to the money which is subscribed, to the Bibles and tracts which are being constantly distributed. They ask us if we really dare to say, in the face of all this, that few are in the way to be saved. In reply, I will only remind these amiable people, that there are other people in the world besides their own little circle, and other men and women besides the chosen few whom they know in their own congregation. I entreat them to open their eyes, and see things as they really are. I assure them there are things going on in this country of ours of which they are at present in happy ignorance. I ask them to sift any parish or congregation in England, with the Bible, before they condemn me hastily. I tell them, if they will do this honestly, they will soon find that I am not far wrong, when I say that few are likely to be saved.

(*d*) I know well that many will not believe me because *they think such a doctrine very narrow-minded and exclusive.* I utterly deny the charge. I disclaim any empathy with those Christians who condemn everybody outside their own communion, and appear to shut the door of heaven against everybody who does not see everything with their eyes. Whether Roman Catholics, or Episcopalians, or Free Churchmen, or Baptists, or Plymouth Brethren, whosoever does anything of this kind, I reckon him an exclusive man. I have no desire to shut up the kingdom of heaven against anyone. All I say is, that none will enter that kingdom, except converted, believing, and holy souls; and all I take on myself to assert is, that both the Bible and facts combine to prove that such persons are few.

(*e*) I know well that many will not believe what I am saying, because *they think it a gloomy, uncharitable doctrine.* It is easy to make vague, general assertions of this kind. It is not so easy to show that any doctrine deserves to be called 'gloomy and uncharitable' which is scriptural and true. There is a spurious charity, I am afraid, which dislikes all strong statements in religion,—a charity which would have no one interfered with,—a charity which would have everyone let alone in his sins,—a charity which, without evidence, takes for granted that everybody is in a way to be saved,—a charity which never doubts that all people are going to heaven, and seems to deny the existence of such a place as hell. But such charity is not the charity of the New Testament, and does not deserve the name. Give me the charity which tries everything by the test of the Bible, and believes nothing, and hopes nothing that is not sanctioned by the Word. Give me the charity which St Paul describes to the Corinthians (1 Cor. 13:1, etc.): the charity which is not blind, and deaf, and stupid, but has eyes to see and senses to discern between him that feareth God and him that feareth him not. Such charity will rejoice in nothing but 'the truth', and will confess with sorrow that I tell nothing but the truth when I say that few are likely to be saved.

(*f*) I know well that many will not believe me, because *they think it presumptuous to have any opinion at all about the number of the saved.* But will these people dare to tell us that the Bible has not spoken plainly as to the character of saved souls? And will they dare to say that there is any standard of truth except the Bible? Surely there can be no presumption in asserting that which is agreeable to the Bible. I tell them plainly that the charge of presumption does not lie at my door. I say that he is the truly presumptuous man who, when the Bible has said a thing clearly and unmistakably, refuses to receive it.

(*g*) I know, finally, that many will not believe me, because *they think my statement extravagant, and unwarrantable.* They regard it as a piece of fanaticism, unworthy of the attention of a rational man. They look on ministers who make such assertions, as weak-minded persons, and wanting in common sense. I can bear such imputations unmoved. I only ask those who make them to show me some plain proof that they are right and I am wrong. Let them show me, if they can, that anybody is likely to get to heaven whose heart is not renewed, who is not a believer in Jesus Christ, who is not a spiritually-minded and holy man. Let them show me, if they can, that people of this description are many, compared with those who are not. Let them, in one word, point to any place on EARTH where the great majority of the people are not ungodly, and the truly godly are not a little flock. Let them do this, and I will grant they have done right to disbelieve what I have said. Till they do this, I must maintain the sorrowful conclusion, that few persons are likely to be saved.

And now it only remains to make some practical application of the subject of this paper. I have set forth as plainly as I can the character of saved people.—I have shown the painful delusions of the world as to the number of the saved.—I have brought forward the evidence of the Bible on the subject.—I have drawn from the world around us plain facts in confirmation of the statements I have made.—May the Lord grant that all these solemn truths may not have been exhibited in vain!

I am quite aware that I have said many things in this paper which are likely to give offence. I know it. It must be so. The point which it handles is far too serious and heart-searching to be otherwise than offensive to some. But I have long had a deep conviction that the subject has been painfully neglected, and that few things are so little realized as the comparative numbers of the lost and saved. All that I have written, I have written because I firmly believe it to be God's truth. All that I have said, I have said, not as an enemy but as a lover of souls. You do not count him an enemy who gives you a bitter medicine to save your life. You do not count him an enemy who shakes you roughly from your sleep when your house is on fire. Surely you will not count me an enemy because I tell you strong truths for the benefit of your soul. I appeal, as a friend, to every man or woman into whose hands this volume has come. Bear with me, for a few moments, while I say a few last words to impress the whole subject on your conscience.

(a) Are there few saved? Then, *shall you be one of the few?* Oh, that you would see that salvation is the one thing needful! Health, and riches, and titles, are not needful things. A man may gain heaven without them. But what shall the man do who dies not saved! Oh, that you would see that you must have salvation now, in this present life, and lay hold upon it for your own soul! Oh, that you would see that 'saved' or 'not saved' is the grand question in religion! High Church or Low Church, Churchman or Dissenter, all these are trifling questions in comparison. What a man needs in order to get to heaven is an actual personal interest in Christ's salvation. Surely, if you are not saved, it will be better at last never to have been born.

(*b*) Are there few saved? Then, *if you are not one of the few already, strive to be one without delay.* I know not who and what you are, but I say boldly, Come to Christ and you shall be saved. The gate that leads to life may be strait, but it was wide enough to admit Manasseh, and Saul of Tarsus, and why not you? The way that leads to life may be narrow, but it is marked by the footsteps of thousands of sinners like yourself. All have found it a good way. All have persevered, and got safe home at last. Jesus Christ invites you. The promises of the gospel encourage you. Oh, strive to enter in without delay!

(*c*) Are there few saved? Then, *if you are doubtful whether you are one of the few, make sure work at once, and be doubtful no more.* Leave no stone unturned in order to ascertain your own spiritual state. Be not content with vague hopes and trusts. Rest not on warm feelings and temporary desires after God. Give diligence to make your calling and election sure. Oh, give me leave to say, that if you are content to live on uncertain about salvation, you live the maddest life in the world! The fires of hell are before you, and you are uncertain whether your soul is insured. This world below must soon be left, and you are uncertain whether you have a mansion prepared to receive you in the world above. The judgment will soon be set, and you are uncertain whether you have an Advocate to plead your cause. Eternity will soon begin, and you are uncertain whether you are prepared to meet God. Oh, sit down this day, and study the subject of salvation! Give God no rest till uncertainty has disappeared, and you have got hold of a reasonable hope that you are saved.

(*d*) Are there few that be saved? Then, *if you are one, be thankful.* Chosen and called of God, while thousands around you are sunk in unbelief,—seeing the kingdom of God, while multitudes around you are utterly blind,—delivered from this present evil world, while crowds are overcome by its love and fear—taught to know sin, and God, and Christ, while numbers, to all appearance as good as you, live in ignorance and darkness,—Oh, you have reason every day to bless and praise God! Whence came this sense of sin, which you now experience? Whence came this love of Christ,—this desire after holiness,—this hungering after righteousness,—this delight in the Word? Has not free grace done it, while many a companion of your youth still knows nothing about it, or has been cut off in his sins? You ought indeed to bless God! Surely Whitefield might well say, that one anthem among the saints in heaven will be 'Why me, Lord? Why didst thou choose me?'

(*e*) Are there few that be saved? Then, *if you are one, do not wonder that you often find yourself standing alone.* I dare believe you are sometimes almost brought to a standstill, by the corruption and wickedness that you see in the world around you. You see false doctrine abounding. You see unbelief and ungodliness of every description. You are sometimes tempted to say, 'Can I really be in the right in my religion? Can it really be that all these people are in the wrong?' Beware of giving way to thoughts like these. Remember, you are only having practical proof of the truth of your Master's sayings. Think not that his purposes are being defeated. Think not that his work is not going forward in the world. He is still taking out a people to his praise. He is still raising up witnesses to himself, here and there, all over the world. The saved will yet be found to be a 'multitude that no man can number', when all are gathered together at last (Rev. 7:9). The earth will yet be filled with the knowledge of the Lord. All nations shall serve him: all kings shall yet delight to do him honour. But the night is not yet spent. The day of the Lord's power is yet to come. In the meantime all is going on as he foretold 1800 years ago. Many are being lost and few saved.

(*f*) Are there few saved? Then, *if you are one, do not be afraid of having too much religion.* Settle it down in your mind that you will aim at the highest degree of holiness, and spiritual-mindedness, and consecration to God,—that you will not be content with any low degree of sanctification. Resolve that, by the grace of God, you will make Christianity beautiful in the eyes of the world. Remember that the children of the world have but few patterns of true religion before them. Endeavour, as far as in you lies, to make those few patterns recommend the service of your Master. Oh, that every true Christian would recollect that he is set as a lighthouse in the midst of a dark world, and would labour so to live that every part of him may reflect light, and no side be dim!

(*g*) Are there few saved? Then, *if you are one, use every opportunity of trying to do good to souls.* Settle it down in your mind that the vast majority of people around you are in awful danger of being lost for ever. Work every engine for bringing the gospel to bear upon them. Help every Christian machinery for plucking brands from the burning. Give liberally to every Society which has for its object to spread the everlasting gospel. Throw all your influence heartily and unreservedly into the cause of doing good to souls. Live like one who thoroughly believes that time is short and eternity near, the devil strong, and sin abounding,—the darkness very great and the light very small,—the ungodly very many and the godly very few;—the things of the world mere transitory shadows, and heaven and hell the great substantial realities. Alas, indeed, for the lives that many believers live! How cold are many, and how frozen,—how slow to do decided things in religion, and how afraid of going *too far*,—how backward to attempt anything new,—how ready to discourage a good movement,—how ingenious in discovering reasons why it is best to sit still,—how unwilling ever to allow that 'the time' for active exertion is come,—how wise in finding fault,—how shiftless in devising plans to meet growing evils! Truly a man might sometimes fancy, when he looks at the ways of many who are counted believers, that all the world was going to heaven, and hell was nothing but a lie.

Let us all beware of this state of mind! Whether we like to believe it or not, hell is filling fast,—Christ is daily holding out his hand to a disobedient people,—many, many are in the way to destruction,—few, few are in the way to life. Many, many are likely to be lost. Few, few are likely to be saved.

Once more I ask every reader, as I asked at the beginning of this paper,—*Shall you be saved?* If you are not saved already, my heart's desire and prayer to God is, that you may seek salvation without delay. If you are saved, my desire is that you may live like a saved soul,—and like one who knows that saved souls are few.

3

Conversion

Repent ye therefore, and be converted.—Acts 3:19.

THE subject which forms the title of this paper is one which touches all mankind. It ought to come home to all ranks and classes, high or low, rich or poor, old or young, gentle or simple. Anyone may get to heaven without money, rank, or learning. No one, however wise, wealthy, noble, or beautiful, will ever get to heaven without CONVERSION.

There are six points of view in which I wish to consider the subject of this paper. I will try to show that conversion is—

    I. *A scriptural thing.*
    II. *A real thing.*
    III. *A necessary thing.*
    IV. *A possible thing.*
    V. *A happy thing.*
    VI. *A thing that may be seen.*

I. Let me show, in the first place, that *conversion is a scriptural thing.*

I mean by this, that conversion is a thing plainly mentioned in the Bible. This is the first point we have to ascertain about anything in religion. It matters nothing who says a thing, and declares it to be religious truth; it matters nothing whether we like or dislike a doctrine. Is it in the Bible? *That* is the only question. If it is, we have no right to refuse it. If we reject a Bible truth because we do not like it, we do so at the peril of our souls, and might as well become infidels at once. This is a principle which ought never to be forgotten.

Let us turn to the Bible. Hear what David says: 'The law of the Lord is perfect, converting the soul'—'Sinners shall be converted unto thee' (Psa. 19:7; 51:13). Hear what our Lord Jesus Christ says: 'Except ye be converted, and become as little children, ye shall not enter into the kingdom of heaven' (Matt. 18:3). Hear what St Peter says: 'Repent ye, and be converted, that your sins may be blotted out' (Acts 3:19). Hear what St James says: 'He which converteth the sinner from the error of his way shall save a soul from death, and shall hide a multitude of sins' (James 5:20).

I could easily add to this scriptural evidence. I could quote many passages in which the *idea* of conversion is contained, though the *word* itself is not used. To be renewed;—to be transformed,—to be created anew,—to be raised from the dead,—to be illuminated,—to pass from death to life;—to be born again,—to put off the old man and put on the new man,—all these are scriptural expressions, which mean the same thing as conversion. They are all the same thing, seen from a different point of view. But enough is as good as a feast, in these matters. There can be no doubt of the truth of my first position,—that conversion is a scriptural thing. It is not a mere device of man's invention: it is in the Bible.

You may tell me, perhaps, that you do not care for 'texts'. You may say that you are not accustomed to make single texts decide questions in your religion. If this is your case, I am sorry for you. Our Lord Jesus Christ and his apostles used to quote single texts frequently, and to make everything in their arguments hinge upon them. One plain text with them was sufficient to settle a point. Is it not a serious matter, that while the Lord Jesus and his apostles made such use of single texts, you do not care for them?

I entreat every reader of these pages to beware of ignorant prejudices on religious subjects. I have known people to find fault with doctrines and opinions as enthusiastic, fanatical, and absurd, in perfect ignorance that they were finding fault with Scripture itself! They have given proof that they spoke of things which they did not understand, and that they knew nothing, comparatively, of the contents of the Bible. It is recorded that, in Somersetshire, one hundred years ago, a great preacher was summoned before the magistrates for swearing in the pulpit. He had used in his sermon the well-known text, 'He that believeth not shall be

damned' (Mark 16:16); and the constable who laid the infor-
mation was so ignorant that he did not know the preacher
was quoting God's Word!—I myself remember a lady of
rank being very indignant, because a speaker at a Mission-
ary meeting described the heathen as 'having no hope'. And
yet the speaker had only used the very expression used by
St Paul, in describing the state of the Ephesians before the
gospel came to them (Eph. 2:12)! Beware of making a like
mistake. Take care that you do not expose your own ignorance by talking against conversion. Search the Scriptures.
CONVERSION IS A SCRIPTURAL THING.

II. Let me show, in the second place, that *conversion is a
real thing*.

I feel it very needful to say something about this point.
We live in an age of shams, cheats, deceptions, and impo-
sitions. It is an age of white-wash, varnish, lacquer, and
veneer. It is an age of plaster, compo, plating, gilding, and
electrotyping. It is an age of adulterated food, paste diamonds, false weights and measures, unsound timber, and
shoddy clothing. It is an age of wind-bags, and whitened
sepulchres, and cymbals in religion. I can hardly wonder
that many regard all Christian professors as suspicious
characters, if not hypocrites, and deny the reality of any
such thing as conversion.

Still, notwithstanding all that such people may say, I assert
confidently, that there is such a thing as conversion. There

are to be seen among men, every here and there, unmistakable cases of a complete turning round of heart, character, tastes, and life,—cases which deserve no other name than that of *conversion*. I say that when a man turns right round from sin to God,—from worldliness to holiness,—from self-righteousness to self-distrust,—from carelessness about religion to deep repentance,—from unbelief to faith,—from indifference to Christ to strong love to Christ,—from neglect of prayer, the Bible, and the Sabbath, to a diligent use of all means of grace,—I say boldly, that such a man is a *converted* man. When a man's heart is turned upside down in the way I have described, so that he loves what he once hated, and hates what he once loved, I say boldly, that it is a case of *conversion*. To deny it, is mere obstinacy and affectation. Such a change can be described in no other way. By far the most suitable name that can be given to it is the scriptural name,—conversion.

Of such changes the Bible gives many unmistakable patterns. Let anyone read attentively the histories of Manasseh King of Judah, of Matthew the apostle, of the woman of Samaria, of Zacchæus the publican, of Mary Magdalene, of Saul of Tarsus, of the Philippian jailer, of Lydia the purple seller, of the Jews to whom Peter preached on the day of Pentecost, of the Corinthians to whom St Paul preached (2 Chron. 33:1-19; Matt. 9:9; John 4:1-29; Luke 19:1-10; 8:2; Acts 9:1-22; 16:14-34; 2:37-41; 1 Cor. 6:9-11). In every one of these cases there was a mighty change. What can that change be called but *conversion*?

Of such changes the history of the church in every age can supply many well-known examples. Let anyone study the life of Augustine, of Martin Luther, of Hugh Latimer, of John Bunyan, of Colonel Gardiner, of John Newton, of Thomas Scott. In every one of these lives he will find a description of a mighty turning of heart, opinion, and conduct, towards God. What can that turning be called better than *conversion*?

Of such changes every man's own neighbourhood and circle of acquaintances will furnish many specimens. Let any honest-minded person of observation look around him, and consider what I assert. Let him deny, if he can, that he can put his finger on men and women of his own age and standing, who are now utterly unlike what they once were in the matter of religion. About their own souls, and the importance of being saved,—about sin, and God, and Christ, and repentance, and faith, and holiness,—about Bible-reading, and praying, and Sabbath-keeping,—about all these things they are completely changed. I challenge any sensible man to deny that he knows such persons. They are to be met with here and there in every part of the kingdom. Once more I ask, what can such changes be called but *conversion*?

I feel almost ashamed to dwell so long on this point. It seems like spending time in proving that two and two make four, or that the sun rises in the east. But, alas, there are too many people who will allow nothing, and will dispute everything, in religion! They know that they are not yet converted themselves, and they therefore try hard to make out that nobody was ever converted at all! I trust I have given a sufficient answer to all such persons. I have shown you that CONVERSION IS A REAL TRUE THING.

III. Let me show, in the third place, that *conversion is a necessary thing*.

This is a point of great importance. Some worthy people are ready enough to admit that conversion is a scriptural truth and a reality, but not a thing which needs to be pressed on most English people. The heathen, they grant, need conversion. Even the thieves, and fallen characters, and inmates of jails, they allow, may require conversion. But to talk of conversion being necessary for church-going people, is to talk of things which they cannot see at all. 'Such people may, in some cases, need a little stirring up and amendment. They may not be quite as good as they ought to be: it would be better if they attended more to religion; but you have no right to say they need conversion! It is uncharitable, harsh, narrow-minded, bitter, wrong, to tell them they require conversion!'

This sadly common notion is a complete delusion. It is a pure invention of man's, without a scrap of foundation in God's Word. The Bible teaches expressly that the change of heart, called *conversion*, is a thing absolutely needed by everyone. It is needed because of the total corruption of human nature. It is needed because of the condition of every man's natural heart. All people born into the world, of every rank and nation, must have their hearts changed between the cradle and the grave, before they can go to heaven. All, all men, without exception, must be converted.

Without conversion of heart *we cannot serve God on earth.* We have naturally neither faith, nor fear, nor love, toward God and his Son Jesus Christ. We have no delight in his Word. We take no pleasure in prayer or communion with him. We have no enjoyment in his ordinances, his house, his people, or his day. We may have a form of Christianity, and keep up a round of ceremonies and religious performances. But without conversion we have no more heart in our religion than a brick or a stone. Can a dead corpse serve God? We know it cannot. Well, without conversion we are dead toward God.

Look round the congregation with which you worship every Sunday. Mark how little interest the great majority of them take in what is going on. Observe how listless, and apathetic, and indifferent, they evidently are about the whole affair. It is clear their hearts are not there! They are thinking of something else, and not of religion. They are thinking of business, or money, or pleasure, or worldly plans, or bonnets, or gowns, or new dresses, or amusements. Their bodies are there, but not their hearts.—And what is the reason? What is it they all need? They need conversion. Without it they only come to church for fashion and form's sake, and go away from church to serve the world or their sins.

But this is not all. Without conversion of heart *we could not enjoy heaven*, if we got there. Heaven is a place where holiness reigns supreme, and sin and the world have no place at all. The company will all be holy; the employments will all be holy; it will be an eternal Sabbath-day. Surely if we go to heaven, we must have a heart in tune and able to enjoy it, or else we shall not be happy. We must have a nature in harmony with the element we live in, and the place where we dwell. Can a fish be happy out of water? We know it cannot. Well, without conversion of heart we could not be happy in heaven.

Look round the neighbourhood in which you live, and the persons with whom you are acquainted. Think what many of them would do if they were cut off for ever from money, and business, and newspapers, and cards, and balls, and races, and hunting, and shooting, and worldly amusements! Would they like it?—Think what they would feel if they were shut up for ever with Jesus Christ, and saints, and angels! Would they be happy?—Would the eternal company of Moses, and David, and St Paul, be pleasant to those who never take the trouble to read what those holy men wrote? Would heaven's everlasting praise suit the taste of those who can hardly spare a few minutes in a week for private religion, even for prayer? There is but one answer to be given to all these questions. We must be *converted* before we can enjoy heaven. Heaven would be no heaven to any child of Adam without conversion.

Let no man deceive us. There are two things which are of absolute necessity to the salvation of every man and woman on earth. One of them is the mediatorial work of Christ *for us*,—his atonement, satisfaction, and intercession. The other is the converting work of the Spirit *in us*,—his guiding, renewing, and sanctifying grace.—We must have both a title and a heart for heaven. Sacraments are only *generally* necessary to salvation: a man may be saved without them, like the penitent thief. An interest in Christ and conversion are *absolutely* necessary: without them no one can possibly be saved.—All, all alike, high or low, rich or poor, old or young, gentle or simple, Churchmen or Dissenters, baptized or unbaptized, all must be converted or perish. There is no salvation without conversion. IT IS A NECESSARY THING.

IV. Let me now show, in the fourth place, that *conversion is a possible thing*.

I think I know the feelings which come across many people's minds, when they read the things which I am writing in this paper. They take refuge in the idea that such a change as conversion is quite impossible, except for a favoured few. 'It is all very well,' they argue, 'for parsons to talk of conversion; but the thing cannot be done; we have work to mind, families to provide for, business to attend to. It is no use expecting miracles now. We cannot be converted.' Such thoughts are very common. The devil loves to put them before us, and our own lazy hearts are only too ready to receive them: but they will not stand examination. I am not afraid to lay it down that conversion is a *possible* thing. If it were not so I would not say another word.

In saying this, however, I should be sorry to be mistaken. I do not for a moment mean that anyone can convert himself, change his own heart, take away his own corrupt nature, put in himself a new spirit. I mean nothing of the kind. I should as soon expect the dry bones in Ezekiel's vision to give themselves life (Ezek. 37:3). I only mean that there is nothing in Scripture, nothing in God, nothing in man's condition, which warrants anyone in saying, 'I can never be converted.' There lives not the man or woman on earth of whom it could be said, 'their conversion is an impossibility.'—Anyone, however sinful and hardened, anyone may be converted.

Why do I speak so confidently? How is it that I can look round the world, and see the desperate wickedness that is in it, and yet despair of no living man's soul? How is it that I can say to anyone, however hard, fallen, and bad, 'Your case is not hopeless: you, even you, may be converted'?—I can do it because of the things contained in Christ's gospel. It is the glory of that gospel that under it nothing is impossible.

Conversion is a possible thing, because of the *almighty power of our Lord Jesus Christ*. In him is life. In his hand are the keys of death and hell. He has all power in heaven

and earth. He quickeneth whom he will (John 1:4; Rev.
1:18; Matt. 28:18; John 5:21). It is as easy to him to create
new hearts out of nothing, as it was to create the world
out of nothing. It is as easy to him to breathe spiritual life
into a stony, dead heart, as it was to breathe natural life
into the clay of which Adam was formed, and make him a
living man. There was nothing he could not do on earth.
Wind, sea, disease, death, the devil,—all were obedient to
his word. There is nothing that he cannot do in heaven at
God's right hand. His hand is as strong as ever: his love is
as great as ever. The Lord Jesus Christ lives, and therefore
conversion is not impossible.

But beside this, conversion is a possible thing, because
of the *almighty power of the Holy Ghost*, whom Christ sends
into the hearts of all whom he undertakes to save. The same
divine Spirit who co-operated with the Father and Son in
the work of creation, co-operates specially in the work of
conversion. It is he who conveys life from Christ, the great
Fountain of Life, into the hearts of sinners. He who moved
on the face of the waters before those wonderful words were
spoken, 'Let there be light,' is he who moves over sinners'
souls, and takes their natural darkness away. Great indeed
is the invisible power of the Holy Ghost! He can soften that
which is hard. He can bend that which is stiff and stubborn. He can give eyes to the spiritually blind, ears to the
spiritually deaf, tongues to the spiritually dumb, feet to the
spiritually lame, warmth to the spiritually cold, knowledge

to the spiritually ignorant, and life to the spiritually dead. 'None teacheth like him!' (Job 36:22). He has taught thousands of ignorant sinners, and never failed to make them 'wise unto salvation'. The Holy Ghost lives, and therefore conversion is never impossible.

What can you say to these things? Away with the idea for ever that conversion is not possible. Cast it behind you: it is a temptation of the devil. Look not at yourself, and your own weak heart—for then you may well despair. Look upward at Christ, and the Holy Ghost, and learn that with them nothing is impossible. Yes! The age of spiritual miracles is not yet past! Dead souls in our congregations can yet be raised; blind eyes can yet be made to see; dumb prayerless tongues can yet be taught to pray. No one ought ever to despair. When Christ has left heaven, and laid down his office as the Saviour of sinners,—when the Holy Ghost has ceased to dwell in hearts, and is no longer God,—then, and not till then, men and women may say, 'We cannot be converted.' Till then, I say boldly, conversion is a possible thing. If men are not converted, it is because they will not come to Christ for life (John 5:40). CONVERSION IS POSSIBLE.

V. Let me show, in the fifth place, that *conversion is a happy thing*.

I shall have written in vain if I leave this point untouched. There are thousands, I firmly believe, who are ready to admit the truth of all I have said hitherto. Scriptural, real, necessary, possible,—all this they willingly allow conversion to be. 'Of course,' they say, 'we know it is all true. People ought to be converted.' But will it increase a man's happiness to be converted? Will it add to a man's joys, and lessen his sorrows, to be converted? Here, alas, is a point at which many stick fast. They have a secret, lurking fear, that if they are converted they must become melancholy, miserable, and low-spirited. Conversion and a sour face,— conversion and a gloomy brow,—conversion and an ill-natured readiness to snub young people, and put down all mirth,—conversion and a sorrowful countenance,—conversion and sighing and groaning,—all these are things which they seem to think must go together! No wonder that such people shrink from the idea of conversion!

The notion I have just described is very common and very mischievous. I desire to protest against it with all my heart, and soul, and mind, and strength. I assert without hesitation, that the conversion described in Scripture is a happy thing, and not a miserable one, and that if converted persons are not happy, the fault must be in themselves. The happiness of a true Christian, no doubt, is not quite of the same sort as that of a worldly man. It is a calm, solid, deep flowing, substantial joy. It is not made up of excitement, levity, and boisterous spasmodic mirth. It is the sober, quiet joy of one who does not forget death, judgment, eternity, and a world to come, even in his chief mirth. But in the main I am confident the converted man is the happiest man.

What says the Scripture? How does it describe the feelings and experience of persons who have been converted? Does it give any countenance to the idea that conversion is a sorrowful and melancholy thing? Let us hear what Levi felt, when he had left the receipt of custom to follow Christ. We read that 'he made a great feast in his own house', as if it was an occasion of gladness (Luke 5:29). Let us hear what Zacchæus the publican felt, when Jesus offered to come to his house. We read that 'he received him joyfully' (Luke 19:6). Let us hear what the Samaritans felt, when they were converted through Philip's preaching. We read that 'there was great joy in that city' (Acts 8:8). Let us hear what the Ethiopian eunuch felt in the day of his conversion. We read that 'he went on his way rejoicing' (Acts 8:39). Let us hear what the Philippian jailer felt in the hour of his conversion. We read that 'he rejoiced, believing in God with all his house' (Acts 16:34). In fact the testimony of Scripture on this subject is always one and the same. Conversion is always described as the cause of joy and not of sorrow, of happiness and not of misery.

The plain truth is that people speak ill of conversion because they know nothing really about it. They run down converted men and women as unhappy, because they judge them by their outward appearance of calmness, gravity, and quietness, and know nothing of their inward peace. They forget that it is not those who boast most of their own performances who do most, and it is not those who talk most of their happiness who are in reality the happiest people.

A converted man is happy, because he has peace with God. His sins are forgiven; his conscience is free from the sense of guilt: he can look forward to death, judgment, and eternity, and not feel afraid. What an immense blessing to feel *forgiven and free*!—He is happy because he finds order in his heart. His passions are controlled, his affections are rightly directed. Everything in his inner man, however weak and feeble, is in its right place, and not in confusion. What an immense blessing *order* is!—He is happy, because he feels independent of circumstances. Come what will, he is provided for: sickness, and losses, and death, can never touch his treasure in heaven, or rob him of Christ. What a blessing to feel *independent*!—He is happy, because he feels ready. Whatever happens he is somewhat prepared: the great business is settled; the great concern of life is arranged. What a blessing to feel *ready*!—These are indeed true springs of happiness. They are springs which are utterly shut up and sealed to an unconverted man.—Without forgiveness of sins, without hope for the world to come, dependent on this world for comfort, unprepared to meet God, he cannot be really happy. Conversion is an essential part of true happiness.

Settle it in your mind today that the friend who labours for your conversion to God is the best friend that you have.

He is a friend not merely for the life to come, but for the life that now is. He is a friend to your present comfort as well as to your future deliverance from hell. He is a friend for time as well as for eternity. CONVERSION IS A HAPPY THING.

VI. Let me now show you, in the last place, that *conversion is a thing that may be seen.*

This is a part of my subject which ought never to be overlooked. Well would it be for the church and the world, if in every age it had received more attention. Thousands have turned away in disgust from religion, because of the wickedness of many who profess it. Hundreds have caused the very name of conversion to stink by the lives they have lived after declaring themselves converted. They have fancied that a few spasmodic sensations and convictions were the true grace of God. They have imagined themselves converted, because their animal feelings were excited. They have called themselves 'converts' without the slightest right or title to that honoured name. All this has done immense harm, and it is doing peculiar harm in the present day. The times demand a very clear assertion of the great principle,—that true conversion is a thing that can always be seen.

I admit fully that the manner of the Spirit's working is invisible. It is like the wind. It is like the attractive power of the magnet. It is like the influence of the moon upon the tides. There is something about it far beyond the reach of man's eyes or understanding.—But while I admit this decidedly, I maintain no less decidedly that the effects of the Spirit's work in conversion will always be seen. Those effects may be weak and feeble at first: to the natural man they may hardly be visible, and not understood. But effects there always will be: some fruit will always be seen where there is true conversion. Where no effect can be seen, there you may be sure there is no grace. Where no visible fruit can be found, there you may be sure is no conversion.

Does anyone ask me what we may expect to see in a true conversion? I reply, There will always be something seen in a converted man's character, and feelings, and conduct, and opinions, and daily life. You will not see in him perfection; but you will see in him something peculiar, distinct, and different from other people. You will see him hating sin, loving Christ, following after holiness, taking pleasure in his Bible, persevering in prayer. You will see him penitent, humble, believing, temperate, charitable, truthful, good-tempered, patient, upright, honourable, kind. These, at any rate, will be his aims: these are the things which he will follow after, however short he may come of perfection. In some converted persons you will see these things more distinctly, in others less. This only I say, wherever there is conversion, something of this kind will be seen.

I care nothing for a conversion which has neither marks nor evidences to show. I shall always say, 'Give me some marks if I am to think you are converted. Show me thy conversion without any marks, if thou canst! I do not believe in it. It is worth nothing at all.'—You may call such doctrine legal if you please. It is far better to be *called* legal than to *be* an Antinomian. Never, never, will I allow that the blessed Spirit can be in a man's heart, when no fruit of the Spirit can be seen in his life. A conversion which allows a man to live in sin, to lie, and drink, and swear, is not the conversion of the Bible. It is a counterfeit conversion, which can only please the devil, and will lead the man who is satisfied with it, not to heaven, but to hell.

Let this last point sink down into your heart and never be forgotten. Conversion is not only a scriptural thing, a real thing, a necessary thing, a possible thing and a happy thing: there remains one more grand characteristic about it,—it is A THING THAT WILL ALWAYS BE SEEN.

And now let me wind up this paper by a few plain appeals to the consciences of all who read it. I have tried to the best of my power to unfold and explain the nature of conversion. I have endeavoured to set it forth in every point of view. Nothing remains but to try to bring it home to the heart of everyone into whose hands this book may fall.

(1) First of all, I urge every reader of this paper to *find out whether he is converted*. I am not asking about other people. The heathen no doubt need conversion. The unhappy inmates of jails and reformatories need conversion. There may be people living near your own house who are open sinners and unbelievers, and need conversion. But all this

is beside the question. I ask, Are you converted yourself?

Are you converted? It is no reply to tell me that many people are hypocrites and false professors. It is no argument to say that there are many sham revivals, and mock conversions. All this may be very true: but the abuse of a thing does not destroy the use of it. The circulation of bad money is no reason why there should not be good coin. Whatever others may be, Are you converted yourself?

Are you converted? It is no answer to tell me that you go to church or chapel, and have been baptized and admitted to the table of the Lord. All this proves little: I could say as much for Judas Iscariot, Demas, Simon Magus, Ananias, and Sapphira. The question is still not answered. Is your heart changed? Are you really converted to God?

(2) In the next place, I urge every reader of this book who is not converted, *never to rest till he is*. Make haste: awake to know your danger. Escape for your life: flee from the wrath to come. Time is short: eternity is near. Life is uncertain: judgment is sure. Arise and call upon God. The throne of grace is yet standing: the Lord Jesus Christ is yet waiting to be gracious. The promises of the gospel are wide, broad, full, and free: lay hold upon them this day. Repent, and believe the gospel: repent, and be converted. Rest not, rest not, rest not, till you know and feel that you are a converted man.

(3) In the last place, I offer a *word of exhortation* to every reader who has reason to think that he has gone through that blessed change of which I have been speaking in this

paper. You can remember the time when you were not what you are now. You can remember a time in your life when old things passed away, and all things became new. To you also I have something to say. Suffer the word of friendly counsel, and lay it to heart.

(*a*) Do you think that you are converted? Then give all diligence to make your calling and conversion sure. Leave nothing uncertain that concerns your immortal soul. Labour to have the witness of the Spirit with your spirit, that you are a child of God. Assurance is to be had in this world, and assurance is worth the seeking. It is good to have hope: it is far better to feel sure.

(*b*) Do you think that you are converted? Then do not expect impossibilities in this world. Do not suppose the day will ever come when you will find no weak point in your heart, no wanderings in private prayer, no distraction in Bible-reading, no cold desires in the public worship of God, no flesh to mortify, no devil to tempt, no worldly snares to make you fall. Expect nothing of the kind. Conversion is not perfection! Conversion is not heaven! The old man within you is yet alive; the world around you is yet full of danger; the devil is not dead. Remember at your best, that a converted sinner is still a poor weak sinner, needing Christ every day. Remember this, and you will not be disappointed.

(*c*) Do you think that you are converted? Then labour and desire to grow in grace every year that you live. Look

97

not to the things behind; be not content with old experience, old grace, old attainments in religion. Desire the sincere milk of the Word, that you may grow thereby (1 Pet. 2:2). Entreat the Lord to carry on the work of conversion more and more in your soul, and to deepen spiritual impressions within you. Read your Bible more carefully every year: watch over your prayers more jealously every year. Beware of becoming sleepy and lazy in your religion. There is a vast difference between the lowest and the highest forms in the school of Christ. Strive to get on in knowledge, faith, hope, charity, and patience. Let your yearly motto be, 'Onward, Forward, Upward!' to the last hour of your life.

(d) Do you think you are converted? Then show the value you place on conversion by your diligence in trying to do good to others.—Do you really believe it is an awful thing to be an unconverted man? Do you really think that conversion is an unspeakable blessing? Then prove it, prove it, prove it, by constant zealous efforts to promote the conversion of others. Look round the neighbourhood in which you live: have compassion on the multitudes who are yet unconverted. Be not content with getting them to come to your church or chapel; aim at nothing less than their entire conversion to God. Speak to them, read to them, pray for them, stir up others to help them. But never, never, if you are a converted man, never be content to go to heaven alone!

4

Justification

*Being justified by faith, we have peace with God through our
Lord Jesus Christ.*—Rom. 5:1.

THERE is a word in the text which heads this page
which ought to be very precious in the eyes of English-
men. That word is '*peace*'.

Even in 'merry England' we have known something of
the horrors of war in the last thirty years. The Crimean war,
the Indian mutiny, the Chinese, Abyssinian, and Ashantee
wars have left deep marks on the history of our country.

We have tasted some of the tremendous evils which war,
however just and necessary, brings in its train. Battle and
disease have done their deadly work among our gallant sol-
diers and sailors. Gentle and simple blood has been shed
like water in far distant lands. Many of the best and brav-
est of our countrymen are lying cold in untimely graves.
Hearts in England have been broken by sudden, stunning,
crushing bereavements. Mourning has been put on in many
a palace, and many a cottage. The light of hundreds of

happy firesides has been quenched. The mirth of thousands of homes is gone. Alas, we have learned by bitter experience what a blessed thing is *peace*!

I desire, however, to call the attention of all who read this paper to the best of all peace,—even peace with God. I would fain speak to you of a peace which this world can neither give nor take away,—a peace which depends on no earthly governments, and needs no carnal weapons, either to win it or preserve it,—a peace which is freely offered by the King of kings, and is within the reach of all who are willing to receive it.

There is such a thing as 'peace with God'. It may be felt and known. My heart's desire and prayer is that you may be able to say with the Apostle Paul, 'Being justified by faith, I have peace with God through our Lord Jesus Christ' (Rom. 5:1).

There are four things which I propose to bring before you, in order to throw light on the whole subject,

I. Let me show you the chief privilege of a true Christian:—*'he has peace with God.'*

II. Let me show you the fountain from which that privilege flows:—*'he is justified.'*

III. Let me show you the rock from which that fountain springs:—*'Jesus Christ.'*

IV. Let me show you the hand by which the privilege is made our own:—*'faith.'*

Upon each of these four points I have something to say. May the Holy Ghost make the whole subject peace-giving to some souls!

I. First of all, let me show the chief privilege of a true Christian:—*he has peace with God.*

When the Apostle Paul wrote his Epistle to the Romans, he used five words which the wisest of the heathen could never have used. Socrates, and Plato, and Aristotle, and Cicero, and Seneca were wise men. On many subjects they saw more clearly than most people in the present day. They were men of mighty minds, and of a vast range of intellect. But not one of them could have said as the apostle did, 'I have peace with God' (Rom. 5:1).

When Paul used these words, he spoke not for himself only, but for all true Christians. Some of them no doubt have a greater sense of this privilege than others. All of them find an evil principle within, warring against their spiritual welfare day by day. All of them find their adversary, the devil, waging an endless battle with their souls. All of them find that they must endure the enmity of the world. But all, notwithstanding, to a greater or less extent, 'have peace with God'.

This peace with God is a calm, intelligent sense of friendship with the Lord of heaven and earth. He that has it, feels as if there was no barrier and separation between himself and his holy Maker. He can think of himself as under the eye of an all-seeing Being and yet not feel afraid. He can believe that this all-seeing Being beholds him, and yet is not displeased.

Such a man can see *death* waiting for him, and yet not be greatly moved. He can go down into the cold river,—close his eyes on all he has on earth,—launch forth into a world unknown, and take up his abode in the silent grave,—and yet feel peace.

Such a man can look forward to the *resurrection* and the judgment, and yet not be greatly moved. He can see with his mind's eye the great white throne,—the assembled world,—the open books,—the listening angels,—the Judge himself,—and yet feel peace.

Such a man can think of *eternity*, and yet not be greatly moved. He can imagine a never-ending existence in the presence of God and of the Lamb,—an everlasting Sunday,—a perpetual communion,—and yet feel peace.

I know of no happiness compared to that which this peace affords. A calm sea after a storm,—a blue sky after a black thunder cloud,—health after sickness,—light after darkness,—rest after toil,—all, all are beautiful and pleasant things. But none, none of them all can give more than a feeble idea of the comfort which those enjoy who have been brought into the state of peace with God. It is 'a peace which passeth all understanding' (Phil. 4:7).

It is *the want* of this very peace which makes many in the world unhappy. Thousands have everything that is thought able to give pleasure, and yet are never satisfied. Their hearts are always aching. There is a constant sense of emptiness within. And what is the secret of all this? They have no peace with God.

It is *the desire* of this very peace which makes many a heathen do much in his idolatrous religion. Hundreds of them have been seen to mortify their bodies, and vex their own flesh in the service of some wretched image which their own hands had made. And why? Because they hungered after peace with God.

It is *the possession* of this very peace on which the value of a man's religion depends. Without it there may be everything to please the eye, and gratify the ear,—forms, ceremonies, services, and sacraments,—and yet no good done to the soul. The grand question that should try all is the state of a man's conscience. Is it peace? *Has he peace with God?*

This is the very peace about which I address every reader of these pages this day. Have you got it? Do you feel it? Is it your own?

If you have it, you are truly *rich*. You have that which will endure for ever. You have treasure which you will not lose when you die and leave the world. You will carry it with you beyond the grave. You will have it and enjoy it to all eternity. Silver and gold you may have none. The praise of man you may never enjoy. But you have that which is far better than either, if you have the peace of God.

If you have it not, you are truly *poor*. You have nothing which will last,—nothing which will wear,—nothing which you can carry with you when your turn comes to die. Naked you came into this world, and naked in every sense you will go forth. Your body may be carried to the grave with pomp and ceremony. A solemn service may be read over your coffin. A marble monument may be put up in your honour. But after all it will be but a pauper's funeral, if you die without PEACE WITH GOD.

II. Let me show you, in the next place, the fountain from which true peace is drawn. *That fountain is justification.*

The peace of the true Christian is not a vague, dreamy feeling, without reason and without foundation. He can show cause for it. He builds upon solid ground. He has peace with God, because he is justified.

Without justification it is impossible to have real peace. Conscience forbids it. Sin is a mountain between a man and God, and must be taken away. The sense of guilt lies heavy on the heart, and must be removed. Unpardoned sin will murder peace. The true Christian knows all this well. His peace arises from a consciousness of his sins being forgiven, and his guilt being put away. His house is not built on sandy ground. His well is not a broken cistern, which can hold no water. He has peace with God, because he is justified.

He is justified, and his sins are *forgiven*. However many, and however great, they are cleansed away, pardoned, and wiped out. They are blotted out of the book of God's remembrance. They are sunk into the depths of the sea.

They are cast behind God's back. They are searched for and not found. They are remembered no more. Though they may have been like scarlet, they are become white as snow; though they may have been red like crimson, they are as wool. And so he has peace.

He is justified and *counted righteous* in God's sight. The Father sees no spot in him, and reckons him innocent. He is clothed in a robe of perfect righteousness, and may sit down by the side of angels without feeling ashamed. The holy law of God, which touches the thoughts and intents of men's hearts, cannot condemn him. The devil, 'the accuser of the brethren', can lay nothing to his charge, to prevent his full acquittal. And so he has peace.

Is he not naturally a poor, weak, erring, defective *sinner*? He is. None knows that better than he does himself. But notwithstanding this, he is reckoned complete, perfect, and faultless before God, for he is justified.

Is he not naturally a *debtor*? He is. None feels that more deeply than he does himself. He owes ten thousand talents, and has nothing of his own to pay. But his debts are all paid, settled, and crossed out for ever, for he is justified.

Is he not naturally liable to the curse of *a broken law*? He is. None would confess that more readily than he would himself. But the demands of the law have been fully satisfied,—the claims of justice have been met to the last tittle, and he is justified.

Does he not naturally *deserve punishment*? He does. None would acknowledge that more fully than he would himself. But the punishment has been borne. The wrath of God against sin has been made manifest. Yet he has escaped, and is justified.

Does anyone who is reading this paper know anything of all this? Are you justified? Do you feel as if you were pardoned, forgiven, and accepted before God? Can you draw near to him with boldness, and say, 'Thou art my Father and my Friend, and I am thy reconciled child'? Oh, believe me, you will never taste true peace until you are *justified*!

Where are your sins? Are they removed and taken away from off your soul? Have they been reckoned for, and accounted for, in God's presence? Oh, be very sure these questions are of the most solemn importance! A peace of conscience not built on justification, is a perilous dream. From such a peace the Lord deliver you!

Go with me in imagination to some of our great London hospitals. Stand with me there by the bedside of some poor creature in the last stage of an incurable disease. He lies quiet perhaps, and makes no struggle. He does not complain of pain perhaps, and does not appear to feel it. He sleeps, and is still. His eyes are closed. His head reclines on his pillow. He smiles faintly, and mutters something. He is dreaming of home, and his mother, and his youth. His thoughts are far away.—But is this health? Oh, no: no! It is only the effect of opiates. Nothing can be done for him.

He is dying daily. The only object is to lessen his pain. His quiet is an unnatural quiet. His sleep is an unhealthy sleep. You see in that man's case a vivid likeness of *peace without justification.* It is a hollow, deceptive, unhealthy thing. Its end is death.

Go with me in imagination to some lunatic asylum. Let us visit some case of incurable delusion. We shall probably find some one who fancies that he is rich and noble, or a king. See how he will take the straw from off the ground, twist it round his head, and call it a crown. Mark how he will pick up stones and gravel, and call them diamonds and pearls. Hear how he will laugh, and sing, and appear to be happy in his delusions.—But is this happiness? Oh, no! We know it is only the result of ignorant insanity. You see in that man's case another likeness of *peace built on fancy, and not on justification.* It is a senseless, baseless thing. It has neither root nor life.

Settle it in your mind that there can be no peace with God, unless we feel that we are justified. *We must know what is become of our sins.* We must have a reasonable hope that they are forgiven, and put away. We must have the witness of our conscience that we are reckoned not guilty before God. Without this it is vain to talk of peace. We have nothing but the shadow and imitation of it. 'There is no peace, saith my God, to the wicked' (Isa. 57:21).

Did you ever hear the sound of the trumpets which are blown before the judges, as they come into a city to open the assizes? Did you ever reflect how different are the feelings which these trumpets awaken in the minds of different men? The innocent man, who has no cause to be tried, hears them unmoved. They proclaim no terrors to him. He listens and looks on quietly, and is not afraid. But often there is some poor wretch, waiting his trial in a silent cell, to whom those trumpets are a knell of despair. They warn him that the day of trial is at hand. Yet a little time and he will stand at the bar of justice, and hear witness after witness telling the story of his misdeeds. Yet a little time, and all will be over,—the trial, the verdict, and the sentence,—and there will remain nothing for him but punishment and disgrace. No wonder the prisoner's heart beats, when he hears that trumpet's sound!

There is a day fast coming when all who are *not justified* shall despair in like manner. The voice of the archangel and the trump of God shall scatter to the winds the false peace which now buoys up many a soul. The day of judgment shall convince thousands of self-willed people too late, that it needs something more than a few beautiful ideas about 'God's love and mercy', to reconcile a man to his Maker, and to deliver his guilty soul from hell. No hope shall stand in that awful day but the hope of the justified man. No peace shall prove solid, substantial, and unbroken, but the peace which is built on *justification*.

Is this peace your own? Rest not, rest not, if you love life, till you know and feel that you are a justified man. Think not that this is a mere matter of names and words. Flatter not yourself with the idea that justification is an 'abstruse and difficult subject', and that you may get to heaven well enough without knowing anything about it. Make up your mind to the great truth that there can be no heaven without peace with God, and no peace with God without justification. And then give your soul no rest till you are a JUSTIFIED MAN.

III. Let me show you, in the third place, the rock from which justification and peace with God flow. *That rock is Christ.*

The true Christian is not justified because of any goodness of his own. His peace is not to be traced up to any work that he has done. It is not purchased by his prayers and regularity, his repentance and his amendment, his morality and his charity. All these are utterly unable to justify him. In themselves they are defective in many things and need a large forgiveness. And as to justifying him, such a thing is not to be named. Tried by the perfect standard of God's law the best of Christians is nothing better than a justified sinner, a pardoned criminal. As to merit, worthiness, desert, or claim upon God's mercy, he has none. Peace built on any such foundations as these is utterly worthless. The man who rests upon them is miserably deceived.

Never were truer words put on paper than those which Richard Hooker penned on this subject 280 years ago. Let those who would like to know what English clergymen thought in olden times, mark well what he says,—'If God would make us an offer thus large, search all the generation of men since the fall of your father Adam, and find *one man*, that hath done any *one action*, which hath past from him pure, without any stain or blemish at all;—and for that one man's one only action, neither man nor angel shall find the torments which are prepared for both:—do you think this ransom, to deliver man and angels, would be found among the sons of men? The best things we do have somewhat in them to be pardoned. How then can we do *anything* meritorious and worthy to be rewarded?'—To these words I desire entirely to subscribe. I believe that no man can be justified by his works before God in the slightest possible degree. Before man he may be justified: his works may evidence the reality of his Christianity. Before God he cannot be justified by anything that he can do: he will be always defective, always imperfect, always short-coming; always far below the mark, so long as he lives. It is not by works of his own that anyone ever has peace and is a justified man.

But how then is a true Christian justified? What is the secret of that peace and sense of pardon which he enjoys? How can we understand a Holy God dealing with a sinful man as with one innocent, and reckoning him righteous notwithstanding his many sins?

The answer to all these questions is short and simple. The true Christian is counted righteous for the sake of Jesus

Christ, the Son of God. He is justified because of the death and atonement of Christ. He has peace because 'Christ died for his sins according to the Scriptures'. This is the key that unlocks the mighty mystery. Here the great problem is solved, how God can be just and yet justify the ungodly. The life and death of the Lord Jesus explain all. 'He is our peace' (1 Cor. 15:3; Eph. 2:14).

Christ has *stood in the place* of the true Christian. He has become his Surety and his Substitute. He undertook to bear all that was to be borne, and to do all that was to be done, and what he undertook he performed. Hence the true Christian is a justified man (Isa. 53:6).

Christ has *suffered for sins,* the 'just for the unjust'. He has endured our punishment in his own body on the cross. He has allowed the wrath of God, which we deserved, to fall on his own head. Hence the true Christian is a justified man (1 Pet. 3:18).

Christ has *paid the debt* the Christian owed, by his own blood. He has reckoned for it, and discharged it to the uttermost farthing by his own death. God is a just God, and will not require his debts to be paid twice over. Hence the true Christian is a justified man (Acts 20:28; 1 Pet. 1:18, 19).

Christ has *obeyed the law* of God perfectly. The devil, the Prince of this World, could find no fault in him. By so fulfilling it he brought in an everlasting righteousness, in which all his people are clothed in the sight of God. Hence the true Christian is a justified man (Dan. 9:24; Rom. 10:4).

Christ, in one word, has lived for the true Christian. Christ has died for him. Christ has gone to the grave for him. Christ has risen again for him. Christ has ascended up on high for him, and gone into heaven to intercede for his soul. Christ has done all, paid all, suffered all that was needful for his redemption. Hence arises the true Christian's justification,—hence his peace. In himself there is nothing, but in Christ he has all things that his soul can require (Col. 2:3; 3:11).

Who can tell the blessedness of the exchange that takes place between the true Christian and the Lord Jesus Christ! Christ's righteousness is placed upon him, and his sins are placed upon Christ. Christ has been reckoned a sinner for his sake, and now he is reckoned innocent for Christ's sake. Christ has been condemned for his sake though there was no fault in him,—and now he is acquitted for Christ's sake, though he is covered with sins, faults, and short-comings. Here is wisdom indeed! God can now be just and yet pardon the ungodly. Man can feel that he is a sinner, and yet have a good hope of heaven and feel peace within. Who among men could have imagined such a thing? Who ought not to admire it when he hears it? (2 Cor. 5:21.)

We read in British history of a Lord Nithsdale who was sentenced to death for a great political crime. He was closely confined in prison after his trial. The day of his execution was fixed. There seemed no chance of escape. And yet before the sentence was carried into effect, he contrived to escape through the skill and affection of his wife. She visited him in prison, and exchanged clothes with him. Dressed in his wife's clothes he walked out of prison and escaped, and neither guards nor keepers detected him, while his wife remained behind in his place. In short, she risked her own life to save the life of her husband. Who would not admire the skill and the love of such a wife as this?

But we read in gospel history of a display of love, compared to which the love of Lady Nithsdale is nothing. We read of Jesus, the Son of God, coming down to a world of sinners, who neither cared for him before he came, nor honoured him when he appeared. We read of him going down to the prison-house, and submitting to be bound, that we the poor prisoners might be able to go free. We read of him becoming obedient to death, and that the death of the cross,—that we the unworthy children of Adam might have a door opened to life everlasting. We read of him being content to bear our sins and carry our transgressions, that we might wear his righteousness, and walk in the light and liberty of the Sons of God (Phil. 2:8).

This may well be called a 'love that passeth knowledge'! In no way could free grace ever have shone so brightly as in the way of *justification by Christ* (Eph. 3:19).

This is *the old way* by which alone the children of Adam, who have been justified from the beginning of the world, have found their peace. From Abel downwards, no man or woman has ever had one drop of mercy excepting through

Christ. To him every altar that was raised before the time of Moses was intended to point. To him every sacrifice and ordinance of the Jewish law was meant to direct the children of Israel. Of him all the prophets testified. In a word, if you lose sight of justification by Christ, a large part of the Old Testament Scripture will become an unmeaning tangled maze.

This, above all, is the way of justification which exactly *meets the wants and requirements of human nature.* There is a conscience left in man, although he is a fallen being. There is a dim sense of his own need, which in his better moments will make itself heard, and which nothing but Christ can satisfy. So long as his conscience is not hungry, any religious toy will satisfy a man's soul and keep him quiet. But once let his conscience become hungry, and nothing will quiet him but real spiritual food and no food but Christ.

There is something within a man when his conscience is really awake, which whispers, *'There must be a price paid for my soul, or no peace.'* At once the gospel meets him with Christ. Christ has already paid a ransom for his redemption. Christ has given himself for him. Christ has redeemed him from the curse of the law, being made a curse for him (Gal. 2:20; 3:13).

There is something within a man, when his conscience is really awake, which whispers, *'I must have some right-eousness or title to heaven, or no peace.'* At once the gospel meets him with Christ. He has brought in an everlasting righteousness. He is the end of the law for righteousness. His name is called the Lord our righteousness. God has made him to be sin for us who knew no sin, that we might be made the righteousness of God in him (2 Cor. 5:21; Rom. 10:4; Jer. 23:6).

There is something within a man, when his conscience is really awake, which whispers, *'There must be punishment and suffering because of my sins, or no peace.'* At once the gospel meets him with Christ. Christ hath suffered for sin, the just for the unjust, to bring him to God. He bore our sins in his own body on the tree. By his stripes we are healed (1 Pet. 2:24; 3:18).

There is something within a man, when his conscience is really awake, which whispers, *'I must have a priest for my soul, or no peace.'* At once the gospel meets him with Christ. Christ is sealed and appointed by God the Father to be the Mediator between himself and man. He is the ordained Advocate for sinners. He is the accredited Counsellor and Physician of sick souls. He is the great High Priest, the Almighty Absolver, the Gracious Confessor of heavy-laden sinners (1 Tim. 2:5; Heb. 8:1).

I know there are thousands of professing Christians who see no peculiar beauty in this doctrine of justification by Christ. Their hearts are buried in the things of the world. Their consciences are palsied, benumbed, and speechless. But whenever a man's conscience begins really to feel and speak, he will see something in Christ's atonement and priestly office which he never saw before. Light does not suit the eye nor music the ear, more perfectly than Christ suits the real wants of a sinful soul. Hundreds can testify that the experience of a converted heathen in the island of Raiatea in the South Pacific Ocean has been exactly their own. 'I saw,' he said, 'an immense mountain, with precipitous sides, up which I endeavoured to climb, but when I had attained a considerable height, I lost my hold and fell to the bottom. Exhausted with perplexity and fatigue, I went to a distance and sat down to weep, and while weeping I saw a drop of blood fall upon that mountain, and in a moment it was dissolved.' He was asked to explain what all this meant. 'That mountain,' he said, 'was my sins, and that drop which fell upon it, was one drop of the precious blood of Jesus, by which the mountain of my guilt was melted away.' (*William's South Sea Missions.*)

This is the one true way of peace,—justification by Christ. Beware lest any turn you out of this way and lead you into any of the false doctrines of the Church of Rome. Alas, it is wonderful to see how that unhappy church has built a house of error hard by the house of truth! Hold fast the truth of God about justification, and be not deceived. Listen not to any thing you may hear about other mediators and helpers to peace. Remember there is no *mediator* but one,—Jesus Christ; no *purgatory* for sinners but one,—the blood of Christ; no *sacrifice* for sin but one,—the sacrifice once made on the cross; no *works* that can merit anything—but the work of Christ; no *priest* that can truly absolve—but Christ. Stand fast here, and be on your guard. Give not the glory due to Christ to another.

What do you know of Christ? I doubt not you have heard of him by the hearing of the ear, and repeated his name in the Belief. You are acquainted perhaps with the story of his life and death. But what experimental knowledge have you of him? What practical use do you make of him? What dealings and transactions have there been between your soul and him?

Oh, believe me, there is *no peace with God excepting through Christ!* Peace is his peculiar gift. Peace is that legacy which he alone had power to leave behind him when he left the world. All other peace beside this is a mockery and a delusion. When hunger can be relieved without food, and thirst quenched without drink, and weariness removed without rest, then, and not till then, will men find peace without Christ.

Now, is this peace your own? Bought by Christ with his own blood, offered by Christ freely to all who are willing to receive it,—is this peace your own? Oh, rest not: rest not till you can give a satisfactory answer to my question,—HAVE YOU PEACE?

IV. Let me show you, in the last place, *the hand by which the privilege of peace is received.*

I ask the special attention of all who read these pages to this part of our subject. There is scarcely any point in

Christianity so important as the means by which Christ, justification, and peace, become the property of a man's soul. Many, I fear, would go with me so far as I have gone in this paper, but would part company here. Let us endeavour to lay hold firmly on the truth.

The means by which a man obtains an interest in Christ and all his benefits is *simple faith*. There is but one thing needful in order to be justified by his blood, and have peace with God. That one thing is to believe on him. This is the peculiar mark of a true Christian. He believes on the Lord Jesus for his salvation. 'Believe on the Lord Jesus Christ and thou shalt be saved.' 'Whosoever believeth in him shall not perish, but have eternal life' (Acts 16:31; John 3:16).

Without this faith it is *impossible to be saved*. A man may be moral, amiable, good-natured, and respectable. But if he does not believe on Christ, he has no pardon, no justification, no title to heaven. 'He that believeth not is condemned already.' 'He that believeth not the Son shall not see life: but the wrath of God abideth on him.' 'He that believeth not shall be damned' (John 3:18, 36; Mark 16:16).

Beside this faith *nothing whatever is needed for a man's justification*. Beyond doubt, repentance, holiness, love, humility, prayerfulness, will always be seen in the justified man. But they do not in the smallest degree justify him in the sight of God. Nothing joins a man to Christ,—nothing justifies, but simple faith. 'To him that worketh not, but believeth on him that justifieth the ungodly, his faith is counted for righteousness.' 'We conclude that a man is justified by faith without the deeds of the law' (Rom. 4:5; 3:28).

Having this faith, a man *is at once completely justified.* His sins are at once removed. His iniquities are at once put away. The very hour that he believes he is reckoned by God entirely pardoned, forgiven, and a righteous man. His justification is not a future privilege, to be obtained after a long time and great pains. It is an immediate present possession. Jesus says, 'He that believeth on me hath everlasting life.' Paul says, 'By him all that believe are justified from all things' (John 6:47; Acts 13:39).

I need hardly say that it is of the utmost importance to have clear views about the nature of true saving faith. It is constantly spoken of as the distinguishing characteristic of New Testament Christians. They are called 'believers'. In the single Gospel of John, 'believing' is mentioned eighty or ninety times. There is hardly any subject about which so many mistakes are made. There is none about which mistakes are so injurious to the soul. The darkness of many a sincere inquirer may be traced up to confused views about faith. Let us try to get a distinct idea of its real nature.

True saving faith is *not the possession of everybody.* The opinion that all who are called Christians are, as a matter of course, believers, is a most mischievous delusion. A man may be baptized, like Simon Magus, and yet have 'no part or lot' in Christ. The visible church contains unbelievers as well as believers. 'All men have not faith' (2 Thess. 3:2).

True saving faith is *not a mere matter of feeling*. A man may have many good feelings and desires in his mind towards Christ, and yet they may all prove as temporary and short-lived as the morning cloud and the early dew. Many are like the stony-ground hearers, and 'receive the word with joy'. Many will say under momentary excitement, 'I will follow thee whithersoever thou goest,' and yet return to the world (Matt. 8:19; 13:20).

True saving faith is *not a bare assent of the intellect* to the fact that Christ died for sinners. This is not a jot better than the faith of devils. They know who Jesus is. 'They believe', and they do more, 'they tremble' (James 2:19).

True saving faith is *an act of the whole inner man*. It is an act of the head, heart, and will, all united and combined. It is an act of the soul, in which,—seeing his own guilt, danger, and hopelessness,—and seeing at the same time Christ offering to save him,—a man ventures on Christ,—flees to Christ,—receives Christ as his only hope,—and becomes a willing dependant on him for salvation. It is an act which becomes at once the parent of a habit. He that has it may not always be equally sensible of his own faith; but in the main he lives by faith, and walks by faith.

True faith has *nothing whatever of merit* about it, and in the highest sense cannot be called 'a work'. It is but laying hold of a Saviour's hand, leaning on a husband's arm, and receiving a physician's medicine. It brings with it nothing to Christ but a sinful man's soul. It gives nothing, contributes nothing, pays nothing, performs nothing. It only receives, takes, accepts, grasps, and embraces the glorious gift of justification which Christ bestows, and by renewed daily acts enjoys that gift.

Of all Christian graces, faith is the most important. Of all, it is the simplest in reality. Of all, it is the most difficult to make men understand in practice. The mistakes into which men fall about it are endless. Some who have no faith never doubt for a moment that they are believers. Others, who have real faith, can never be persuaded that they are believers at all. But nearly every mistake about faith may be traced up to the old root of natural pride. Men will persist in sticking to the idea that they are to pay something of their own in order to be saved. As to a faith which consists in receiving only, and paying nothing at all, it seems as if they could not understand it.

Saving faith is the *hand* of the soul. The sinner is like a drowning man at the point of sinking. He sees the Lord Jesus Christ holding out help to him. He *grasps* it and is saved. This is faith (Heb. 6:18).

Saving faith is the *eye* of the soul. The sinner is like the Israelite bitten by the fiery serpent in the wilderness, and at the point of death. The Lord Jesus Christ is offered to him as the brazen serpent, set up for his cure. He *looks* and is healed. This is faith (John 3:14, 15).

Saving faith is the *mouth* of the soul. The sinner is starving for want of food, and sick of a sore disease. The Lord

Jesus Christ is set before him as the bread of life, and the universal medicine. He *receives* it, and is made well and strong. This is faith (John 6:35).

Saving faith is the *foot* of the soul. The sinner is pursued by a deadly enemy, and is in fear of being overtaken. The Lord Jesus Christ is put before him as a strong tower, a hiding place, and a refuge. He *runs* into it and is safe. This is faith (Prov. 18:10).

If you love life cling with a fast hold to the doctrine of justification by faith. If you love inward peace, let your views of faith be very simple. Honour every part of the Christian religion. Contend to the death for the necessity of holiness. Use diligently and reverently every appointed means of grace: but do not give to these things the office of *justifying* your soul in the slightest degree. If you would have peace, and keep peace, remember that faith alone justifies, and that not as a meritorious work, but as the act that joins the soul to Christ. Believe me, the crown and glory of the gospel is justification by faith without the deeds of the law.

No doctrine can be imagined *so beautifully simple* as justification by faith. It is not a dark mysterious truth, intelligible to none but the great, the rich, and the learned. It places eternal life within the reach of the most unlearned, and the poorest in the land. It must be of God.

No doctrine can be imagined *so glorifying to God*. It honours all his attributes, his justice, mercy, and holiness. It gives the whole credit of the sinner's salvation to the

Saviour he has appointed. It honours the Son, and so honours the Father that sent him (John 5:23). It gives man no partnership in his redemption, but makes salvation to be wholly of the Lord. It must be of God.

No doctrine can be imagined *so calculated to put man in his right place.* It shows him his own sinfulness, and weakness, and inability to save his soul by his own works. It leaves him without excuse if he is not saved at last. It offers to him peace and pardon 'without money and without price'. It must be of God (Isa. 55:1).

No doctrine can be imagined *so comforting to a broken-hearted and penitent sinner.* It brings to such an one glad tidings. It shows him that there is hope even for him. It tells him, though he is a great sinner, there is ready for him a great Saviour; and though he cannot justify himself, God can and will justify him for the sake of Christ. It must be of God.

No doctrine can be imagined *so satisfying to a true Christian.* It supplies him with a solid ground of comfort,—the finished work of Christ. If anything was left for the Christian to do, where would his comfort be? He would never know that he had done enough, and was really safe. But the doctrine that Christ undertakes all, and that we have only to believe and receive peace, meets every fear. It must be of God.

No doctrine can be imagined *so sanctifying.* It draws men by the strongest of all cords, the cord of love. It makes them feel they are debtors, and in gratitude bound to love much, when much has been forgiven. Preaching up works never produces such fruit as preaching them down. Exalting man's goodness and merits never makes men so holy as exalting Christ. The fiercest lunatics at Paris became gentle, mild, and obedient, when Abbé Pinel gave them liberty and hope. The free grace of Christ will produce far greater effects on men's lives than the sternest commands of law. Surely the doctrine must be of God.

No doctrine can be imagined *so strengthening to the hands of a minister*. It enables him to come to the vilest of men, and say, 'There is a door of hope even for you.' It enables him to feel, 'While life lasts there are no incurable cases among the souls under my charge.' Many a minister by the use of this doctrine can say of souls, 'I found them in the state of nature. I beheld them pass into the state of grace. I watched them moving into the state of glory.' Truly this doctrine must be of God.

No doctrine can be imagined that *wears so well*. It suits men when they first begin, like the Philippian jailer, crying, 'What shall I do to be saved?'—It suits them when they fight in the forefront of the battle. Like the Apostle Paul, they say, 'The life that I live, I live by the faith of the Son of God' (Gal. 2:20).—It suits them when they die, as it did Stephen when he cried, 'Lord Jesus, receive my spirit' (Acts 7:59).—Yes: many an one has opposed the doctrine fiercely while he lived, and yet on his deathbed has gladly embraced justification by faith, and departed saying that '*he trusted in nothing but Christ*'. It must be of God.

Have you this faith? Do you know any thing of simple child-like confidence in Jesus? Do you know what it is to rest your soul's hopes wholly on Christ? Oh, remember that where there is no faith, there is no interest in Christ;—where there is no interest in Christ, there is no justification,—where there is no justification, there can be no peace with God;—where there is no peace with God, there is no heaven! And what then? There remains nothing but hell.

And now, let me commend the solemn matters we have been considering to the serious and prayerful attention of all who read this paper. I invite you to begin by meditating calmly on peace with God,—on justification,—on Christ,—on faith. These are not mere speculative subjects, fit for none but retired students. They lie at the very roots of Christianity. They are bound up with life eternal. Bear with me for a few moments, while I add a few words in order to bring them home more closely to your heart and conscience.

1. Let me, then, for one thing, request every reader of this paper to put *a plain question* to himself.

Have you peace with God? You have heard of it. You have read of it. You know there is such a thing. You know where it is to be found. But do you possess it yourself? Is it yet your own? Oh, deal honestly with yourself, and do not evade my question! *Have you peace with God?*

I do not ask whether you think it an excellent thing, and hope to procure it at some future time before you die. I want to know about your state now. Today, while it is called today, I ask you to deal honestly with my question. *Have you peace with God?*

Do not, I beseech you, allow any public events to make you put off the consideration of your own spiritual welfare. The wars and contentions of nations will never cease. The strife of political parties will never end. But after all, a hundred years hence these very things will seem of little importance to you. The question I am asking will seem a thousand times more important. You may possibly be saying then, too late, *'Oh, that I had thought more about peace with God!'*

May the question ring in your ears, and never leave you till you can give it a satisfactory answer! May the Spirit of God so apply it to your heart that you may be able to say boldly, before you die, 'Being justified by faith, I have peace with God through Jesus Christ our Lord!'

2. In the next place, let me offer *a solemn warning* to every reader of this paper who knows that he has not peace with God.

You have not peace! Consider for a moment how fearfully great is your *danger*! You and God are not friends. The wrath of God abideth on you. God is angry with you every day. Your ways, your words, your thoughts, your actions, are a continual offence to him. They are all unpardoned and unforgiven. They cover you from head to foot. They provoke him every day to cut you off. The sword that the reveller of old saw hanging over his head by a single hair, is but a faint emblem of the danger of your soul. There is but a step between you and hell.

You have not peace! Consider for a moment how fearfully great is your *folly*! There sits at the right hand of God a mighty Saviour able and willing to give you peace, and you do not seek him. For ten, twenty, thirty, and perhaps forty years he has called to you, and you have refused his counsel. He has cried, 'Come to me,' and you have practically replied, 'I will not.' He has said, 'My ways are ways of pleasantness,' and you have constantly said, 'I like my own sinful ways far better.'

And after all, for what have you refused Christ? For worldly riches, which cannot heal a broken heart,—for worldly business, which you must one day leave,—for worldly pleasures, which do not really satisfy: for these things, and such as these, you have refused Christ! Is this wisdom! is this fairness, is this kindness to your soul?

I do beseech you to consider your ways. I mourn over your present condition with especial sorrow. I grieve to think how many are within a hair's breadth of some crushing affliction, and yet utterly unprepared to meet it. Fain would I draw near to everyone, and cry in his ear, 'Seek Christ! Seek Christ, that you may have peace within and a present help in trouble.' Fain would I persuade every anxious parent and wife and child to become acquainted with him, who is a brother born for adversity, and the Prince of peace,—a friend that never fails nor forsakes, and a husband that never dies.

3. Let me, in the next place, offer *an affectionate entreaty* to all who want peace and know not where to find it.

You want peace! Then seek it without delay from him who alone is able to give it,—Christ Jesus the Lord. Go to him in humble prayer, and ask him to fulfil his own promises and look graciously on your soul. Tell him you have read his compassionate invitation to the 'labouring and heavy laden'. Tell him that this is the plight of your soul, and implore him to give you rest. Do this, and do it without delay.

Seek Christ himself, and *do not stop short of personal dealings with him*. Rest not in regular attendance on Christ's ordinances. Be not content with becoming a communicant, and receiving the Lord's supper. Think not to find solid peace in this way. You must see the King's face, and be touched by the golden sceptre. You must speak to the Physician, and open your whole case to him. You must be closeted with the Advocate, and keep nothing back from him. Oh, remember this! Many are shipwrecked just outside the harbour. They stop short in means and ordinances, and never go completely to Christ. 'Whosoever drinks of this water shall thirst again' (John 4:13). Christ himself can alone satisfy the soul.

Seek Christ, and *wait for nothing*. Wait not till you feel you have repented enough. Wait not till your knowledge is increased. Wait not till you have been sufficiently humbled because of your sins. Wait not till you have no ravelled tangle of doubts and darkness and unbelief all over your heart. Seek Christ just as you are. You will never be better by keeping away from him. From the bottom of my heart I subscribe to old Traill's opinion, *'It is impossible that people should believe in Christ too soon.'* Alas, it is not humility, but pride and ignorance that make so many anxious souls hang back from closing with Jesus. They forget that the more sick a man is, the more need he has of the physician. The more bad a man feels his heart, the more readily and speedily ought he to flee to Christ.

Seek Christ, and *do not fancy you must sit still.* Let not Satan tempt you to suppose that you must wait in a state of passive inaction, and not strive to lay hold upon Jesus. How you can lay hold upon him I do not pretend to explain. But I am certain that it is better to struggle towards Christ and strive to lay hold, than to sit still with our arms folded in sin and unbelief. Better perish striving to lay hold on Jesus, than perish in indolence and sin. Well says old Traill, of those who tell us they are anxious but cannot believe in Christ: 'This pretence is as inexcusable as if a man wearied with a journey, and not able to go one step further, should argue, *"I am so tired that I am not able to lie down,"* when indeed he can neither stand nor go.'

4. Let me, in the next place, offer *some encouragement* to those who have good reason to hope they have peace with God, but are troubled by doubts and fears.

You have doubts and fears! But what do you expect? What would you have? Your soul is married to a body full of weakness, passions, and infirmities. You live in a world that lies in wickedness, a world in which the great majority do not love Christ. You are constantly liable to the temptations of the devil. That busy enemy, if he cannot shut you out of heaven, will try hard to make your journey uncomfortable. Surely all these things ought to be considered.

I say to every believer, that so far from being surprised that you have doubts and fears, I should suspect the reality of your peace if you had none. I think little of that grace which is accompanied by no inward conflict. There is seldom life in the heart when all is still, quiet, and in one way of thinking. Believe me, a true Christian may be known by his *warfare* as well as by his peace. These very doubts and fears which now distress you are tokens of good. They satisfy me that you have really got something which you are afraid to lose.

Beware that you do not help Satan by becoming an unjust accuser of yourself, and an unbeliever in the reality of God's work of grace. I advise you to pray for more knowledge of your own heart, of the fulness of Jesus, and of the devices of the devil. Let doubts and fears drive you to the throne of grace, stir you up to more prayer, send you more frequently to Christ. But do not let doubts and fears rob you of your peace. Believe me, you must be content to go to heaven as a sinner saved by grace. And you must not be surprised to find daily proof that you really are a sinner so long as you live.

5. Let me, in the last place, offer *some counsel* to all who have peace with God, and desire to keep up a lively sense of it.

It must never be forgotten that a believer's sense of his own justification and acceptance with God admits of many degrees and variations. At one time it may be bright and clear; at another dull and dim. At one time it may be high and full, like the flood tide; at another low, like the ebb. Our justification is a fixed, changeless, immovable thing. But our *sense* of justification is liable to many changes.

What then are the best means of preserving in a believer's heart that lively sense of justification which is so precious to the soul that knows it? I offer a few hints to believers. I lay no claim to infallibility in setting down these hints, for I am only a man. But such as they are I offer them.

(*a*) To keep up a lively sense of peace, there must be constant *looking to Jesus*. As the pilot keeps his eye on the mark by which he steers, so must we keep our eye on Christ.

(*b*) There must be constant *communion with Jesus*. We must use him daily as our soul's Physician, and High Priest. There must be daily conference, daily confession, and daily absolution.

(*c*) There must be constant *watchfulness* against the enemies of your soul. He that would have peace must be always prepared for war.

(*d*) There must be constant *following after holiness* in every relation of life,—in our tempers, in our tongues, abroad and at home. A small speck on the lens of a telescope is enough to prevent our seeing distant objects clearly. A little dust will soon make a watch go incorrectly.

(*e*) There must be a constant *labouring after humility*. Pride goes before a fall. Self-confidence is often the mother of sloth, of hurried Bible-reading, and sleepy prayers. Peter first said he would never forsake his Lord, though all others did;—then he slept when he should have prayed;—then he denied him three times, and only found wisdom after bitter weeping.

(*f*) There must be constant *boldness in confessing* our Lord before men. Them that honour Christ, Christ will honour with much of his company. When the disciples forsook our Lord they were wretched and miserable. When they confessed him before the council, they were filled with joy and the Holy Ghost.

(*g*) There must be constant *diligence about means of grace*. Here are the ways in which Jesus loves to walk. No disciple must expect to see much of his Master, who does not delight in public worship, Bible-reading, and private prayer.

(*h*) Lastly, there must be constant *jealousy* over our own souls, and frequent self-examination. We must be careful to distinguish between justification and sanctification. We must beware that we do not make a Christ of holiness.

I lay these hints before all believing readers. I might easily add to them. But I am sure they are among the first things to be attended to by true Christian believers, if they wish to keep up a lively sense of their own justification and acceptance with God.

I conclude all by expressing my heart's desire and prayer that all who read these pages may know what it is to have the peace of God which passeth all understanding in their souls.

If you never had 'peace' yet, may it be recorded in the book of God that this year you sought peace in Christ and found it!

If you have tasted 'peace' already, may your sense of peace mightily increase!

***

The following passage from a direction for the Visitation of the Sick, composed by Anselm, Archbishop of Canterbury, about the year 1093, will probably be interesting to many readers.

Dost thou believe that thou canst not be saved but by the death of Christ? The sick man answereth, Yes. Then let it be said unto him, Go to then, and whilst thy soul abideth in thee, put all thy confidence in this death alone. Place thy trust in no other thing. Commit thyself wholly to this death. Cover thyself wholly with this alone. Cast thyself wholly on this death. Wrap thyself wholly in this death.

And if God would judge thee, say, 'Lord, I place the death of our Lord Jesus Christ between me and thy judgment; and otherwise I will not contend with thee.' And if he shall say unto thee that thou art a sinner, say, 'I place the death of our Lord Jesus Christ between me and my sins.' If he shall say unto thee that thou hast deserved damnation, say, 'Lord, I put the death of our Lord Jesus Christ between thee and all my sins; and I offer his merits for my own, which I should have, and have not.' If he say that he is angry with thee, say, 'Lord, I place the death of our Lord Jesus Christ between me and thy anger.'—*Quoted by Owen in his Treatise on Justification.* (Johnstone's Edition of Owen's Works. Vol. V, p. 17.)[1]

[1] Repr. Edinburgh: Banner of Truth Trust, 2007.

5

The Holy Spirit

If any man have not the Spirit of Christ, he is none of his.
—Rom. 8:9.

THE subject of this paper is one of the deepest importance to our souls. That subject is the work of God the
Holy Ghost. The solemn words of the text which heads this
page demand the attention of all who believe the Scriptures
to be the living voice of God. 'If any man have not the Spirit
of Christ, he is NONE OF HIS.'

It is probable that most of those into whose hands this
paper will fall, have been baptized. And in what name were
you baptized? It was 'In the name of the Father, and of the
Son, and of the Holy Ghost'.

It is probable that many readers of this paper are married
people. And in what name were you pronounced man and
wife together? Again, it was 'In the name of the Father, and
of the Son, and of the Holy Ghost'.

It is not unlikely that many readers of this paper are
members of the Church of England. And in what do you

declare your belief every Sunday, when you repeat the Creed? You say that you 'Believe in God the Father, and in God the Son, and in God the Holy Ghost'.

It is likely that many readers of this paper will be buried one day with the burial service of the Church of England. And what will be the last words pronounced over your coffin, before the mourners go home, and the grave closes over your head? They will be, 'The grace of our Lord Jesus Christ, and the love of God, and the fellowship of the Holy Ghost be with you all' (2 Cor. 13:14).

Now I ask every reader of this paper a plain question: Do you know what you mean by these words, so often repeated,—the Holy Ghost?—What place has God the Holy Ghost in your religion?—What do you know of his office, his work, his indwelling, his fellowship, and his power?—This is the subject to which I ask your attention this day. I want you to consider seriously what you know about the work of God the Holy Ghost.

I believe that the times in which we live demand frequent and distinct testimonies upon this great subject. I believe that few truths of the Christian religion are so often obscured and spoiled by false doctrine as the truth about the Holy Ghost. I believe that there is no subject which an ignorant world is so ready to revile as 'cant, fanaticism, and enthusiasm', as the subject of the work of the Holy Ghost. My heart's desire and prayer to God is, that about this subject I may write nothing but the 'truth as it is in Jesus', and that I may write that truth in love.

For convenience sake I shall divide my subject into four heads. I shall examine in order:—

I. Firstly,—the *importance* attached to the work of the Holy Ghost in Scripture.

II. Secondly,—the *necessity* of the work of the Holy Ghost to man's salvation.

III. Thirdly,—the *manner* in which the Holy Ghost works in man's heart.

IV. Lastly,—the *marks and evidences* by which the presence of the Holy Ghost in a man's heart may be known.

I. The first point I propose to consider is *the importance attached to the work of the Holy Ghost in Scripture.*

I find it hard to know where to begin and where to leave off, in handling this branch of my subject. It would be easy to fill up all this paper by quoting texts about it. So often is the Holy Ghost mentioned in the New Testament, that my difficulty is not so much the discovery of evidence as the selection. Eighteen times in the eighth chapter of the Epistle to the Romans St Paul speaks of God the Spirit. In fact the place which the Holy Ghost holds in the minds of most professing Christians bears no proportion to the place which he holds in the Word.[1]

[1] 'There is a general omission in the saints of God, in their not giving the Holy Ghost that glory that is due to his Person, and for his great work of salvation in us; insomuch that we have in our hearts almost lost this Third Person. We give daily in our thoughts, prayers, affections and speeches, an honour to the Father

I shall not spend much time in proving the divinity and personality of the Holy Ghost. They are points which are written in Scripture as with a sun-beam. I am utterly at a loss to understand how any honest-minded reader of the Bible can fail to see them. Above all, I am unable to comprehend how any unprejudiced reader of the Bible can regard the Spirit as nothing more than 'an influence or principle'. We find it written in the New Testament, that the Holy Ghost was 'seen descending in a bodily shape' (Luke 3:22). He commanded disciples to do acts, and lifted them through the air by his own power (Acts 8:29-39). He sent forth the first preachers to the Gentiles (Acts 13:2). He spake to the churches (Rev. 2:7). He maketh intercession (Rom. 8:26). He searcheth all things, teacheth all things, and guideth into all truth (1 Cor. 2:10; John 14:26; 16:13). He is another Comforter distinct from Christ (John 14:16). He has personal affections ascribed to him (Isa. 63:10; Eph. 4:30; Rom. 15:30). He has a mind, will, and power of his own (Rom. 8:27; 1 Cor. 12:11; Rom. 15:13). He has baptism administered in his name together with the Father and the Son (Matt. 28:19). And whosoever shall blaspheme him hath never forgiveness, and is in danger of eternal damnation (Mark 3:29).

---

and the Son. But who directs the aims of his praise (more than in that general way of doxology we use to close our prayers with) unto God the Holy Ghost? He is a Person in the Godhead, equal with the Father and the Son. The work he doth for us, in its kind, is as great as those of the Father or the Son. Therefore, by the equity of all law, a proportionable honour is due to him.'—*Thomas Goodwin on the Work of the Holy Ghost.* 1704.

I make no comment on these passages. They speak for themselves. I only use the words of Ambrose Serle in saying, that 'Two and two making four, does not appear more clear and conclusive than that the Holy Spirit is a living divine Agent, working with consciousness, will, and power. If people will not be persuaded by these testimonies, neither would they be persuaded though one rose from the dead.'[2]

I repeat that I will not spend time in dwelling on proofs of the Holy Spirit's divinity and personality. I will rather confine all I have to say on this branch of my subject to two general remarks.

For one thing, I ask my readers to remark carefully that *in every step of the grand work of man's redemption the Bible assigns a prominent place to God the Holy Ghost.*

What do you think of the incarnation of Christ? You know we cannot over-rate its importance. Well! it is written that when our Lord was conceived of the Virgin Mary, 'the Holy Ghost came upon her, and the power of the Highest overshadowed her' (Luke 1:35).

What do you think of the earthly ministry of our Lord Jesus Christ? You know that none ever did what he did, lived as he lived, and spake as he spake. Well! it is written that the Spirit 'descended from heaven like a dove and abode upon him',—that 'God anointed him with the Holy Ghost',—that 'the Father gave not the Spirit by measure

---

[2] Serle's *Horæ Solitariæ*.

unto him', and that he was 'full of the Holy Ghost' (John 1:32; Acts 10:38; John 3:34; Luke 4:1).

What do you think of the vicarious sacrifice of Christ on the cross? Its value is simply unspeakable. No wonder St Paul says, 'God forbid that I should glory, save in the cross' (Gal. 6:14). Well! it is written, 'Through the eternal Spirit he offered himself without spot to God' (Heb. 9:14).

What do you think of the resurrection of Christ? It was the seal and top-stone of all his work. He was 'raised again for our justification' (Rom. 4:25). Well! it is written that 'He was put to death in the flesh, but quickened by the Spirit' (1 Pet. 3:18).

What do you think of the departure of Christ from this world, when he ascended up into heaven? It was a tremendous trial to his disciples. They were left like a little orphan family, in the midst of cruel enemies. Well! what was the grand promise wherewith our Saviour cheered them the night before he died? 'I will pray the Father and he shall give you another Comforter, even the Spirit of truth' (John 14:16, 17).

What do you think of the mission of the apostles to preach the gospel? We Gentiles owe to it all our religious light and knowledge. Well! they were obliged to tarry at Jerusalem and 'wait for the promise of the Father'. They were unfit to go forth till they were 'filled with the Holy Ghost', upon the day of Pentecost (Acts 1:4; 2:4).

What do you think of the Scripture, which is written for

our learning? You know that our earth without a sun would be but a faint emblem of a world without a Bible. Well! we are informed that in writing that Scripture, 'Holy men spake as they were moved by the Holy Ghost' (2 Pet. 1:21). 'The things which we speak,' says St Paul, 'we speak in the words which the Holy Ghost teacheth' (1 Cor. 2:13).

What do you think of the whole dispensation under which we Christians live? You know its privileges as far exceed those of the Jews as twilight is exceeded by noonday. Well! we are especially told that it is the 'ministration of the Spirit' (2 Cor. 3:8).[3]

I place these texts before my readers as matter for private meditation. I pass on to the other general remark I promised to make.

I ask you then to remark carefully, that *whatever individual Christians have, are, and enjoy, in contradistinction to the worldly and unconverted, they owe to the agency of God the Holy Ghost.* By him they are first called, quickened, and made alive. Of him they are born again, and made new creatures. By him they are convinced of sin, guided into all truth and led to Christ. By him they are sealed unto the day

---

[3] I would not for a moment have anyone suppose that I think Old Testament believers had not the Holy Ghost. On the contrary I hold that there has never been a whit of spiritual life among men, excepting from the Holy Ghost,—and that the Holy Ghost made Abel and Noah what they were no less really than he made St Paul. All I mean to assert is, that the Holy Ghost is so much more fully revealed and largely poured out under the New Testament than under the Old, that the New Testament dispensation is emphatically and peculiarly called the 'ministration of the Spirit'. The difference between the two dispensations is only one of degree.

of redemption. He dwells in them as his living temples. He witnesses with their spirits,—gives them the spirit of adoption, makes them to cry 'Abba, Father', and makes intercession for them. By him they are sanctified. By him the love of God is shed abroad in their hearts. Through his power they abound in hope. Through him they wait for the hope of righteousness by faith. Through him they mortify the deeds of their bodies. After him they walk. In him they live. In a word, all that believers have from grace to glory,—all that they are from the first moment they believe to the day they depart to be with Christ,—all, all, all may be traced to the work of God the Holy Ghost (John 6:63; 3:8; 16:8-11; Eph. 4:30; 1 Cor. 6:19; Rom. 8:15, 16, 26; 2 Thess. 2:13; Rom. 5:5; 15:13; Gal. 5:5, 25; Rom. 8:1, 13).

I may not tarry longer on this branch of my subject. I trust I have said enough to prove that I did not use words without meaning when I spoke of the importance attached in Scripture to the work of the Spirit of God.

Before I pass on let me entreat all who read this paper to make sure that they hold sound doctrine concerning the word of the Holy Ghost.[4] Give him the honour due unto his name. Give him in your religion the place and the dignity which Scripture assigns to him. Settle it in your minds that the work of all three Persons in the Blessed Trinity, is absolutely and equally needful to the

---

[4] 'To give the Holy Spirit divine worship, if he be not God, is idolatry; and to withhold it, if he is God, is a heinous sin. To be well informed on this point, is of the last importance.'—*Hurrion on the Holy Spirit.* 1731.

salvation of every saved soul. The election of God the Father, and the atoning blood of God the Son, are the foundation stones of our faith. But from them must never be separated the applicatory work of God the Holy Ghost. The Father chooses. The Son mediates, absolves, justifies, and intercedes. The Holy Ghost applies the whole work to man's soul. Always together in Scripture, never separated in Scripture, let the offices of the three Persons in the Trinity never be wrenched asunder and disjoined in your Christianity. What God hath so beautifully joined together let no man dare to put asunder.

Accept a brotherly caution against all kinds of Christian teaching, falsely so called, which, either directly or indirectly, dishonour the work of the Holy Ghost. Beware of *the error, on one side*, which practically substitutes church membership and participation of the sacraments for the Spirit. Let no man make you believe that to be baptized and to go to the Lord's table, is any sure proof that you have the Spirit of Christ.—Beware of *the error, on the other side*, which proudly substitutes the inward light, so called, and the scraps of conscience which remain in every man after the fall, for the saving grace of the Holy Spirit.[5] Let no man

---

[5] 'It is not the natural light of conscience, nor that improved by the Word, which converts any man to God, although this is the best spring of most men's practical part of religion. But it is faith, bringing in a new light into conscience, and so conscience lighting its taper at that sun which humbleth for sin in another manner, and drives men to Christ, sanctifieth, changeth, and writes the law in the heart. And this you will find to be the state of difference between Augustine, and the Pelagians, and Semi-Pelagians, which the whole stream and current of

make you believe that as a matter of course, since Christ died, all men and women have within them the Spirit of Christ.—I touch on these points gently. I should be sorry to write one needless word of controversy. But I do say to everyone who prizes real Christianity in these days, 'Be very jealous about the real work and office of the third Person of the Trinity.' Try the spirits whether they be of God. Prove diligently the many divers and strange doctrines which now infect the church. And let the subject brought before you this day be one of your principal tests. Try every new doctrine of these latter times by two simple questions. Ask first, 'Where is the Lamb?' And ask secondly, 'Where is the Holy Ghost?'

II. The second point I propose to consider, is *the necessity of the work of the Holy Ghost to man's salvation.*

I invite special attention to this part of the subject. Let it be a settled thing in our minds that the matter we are considering in this paper is no mere speculative question in religion, about which it signifies little what we believe. On the contrary, it lies at the very foundation of all saving Christianity. Wrong about the Holy Ghost and his offices,

---

his writings against them hold forth. They would have had the light of natural conscience, and the seeds of natural virtues in men (as in philosophers), being improved and manured by the revelation of the Word, to be that grace which the Scripture speaks of. He proclaims all their virtues, and their use of natural light to be sins, because deficient of holiness, and requires for us not only the revelation of the objects of faith, which else natural light could not find out, but a new light to see them withal.'—*Thomas Goodwin on the Work of the Holy Ghost.* 1704.

we are wrong to all eternity.

The necessity of the work of the Holy Ghost arises from the total corruption of human nature. We are all by nature 'dead in sins' (Eph. 2:1). However shrewd, and clever, and wise in the things of this world, we are all dead towards God. The eyes of our understanding are blinded. We see nothing aright. Our wills, affections, and inclinations are alienated from him who made us. 'The carnal mind is enmity against God' (Rom. 8:7). We have naturally neither faith, nor fear, nor love, nor holiness. In short, left to ourselves, we should never be saved.

Without the Holy Ghost *no man ever turns to God, repents, believes, and obeys.*—Intellectual training and secular education alone make no true Christians. Acquaintance with fine arts and science leads no one to heaven. Pictures and statues never brought one soul to God. The 'tender strokes of art' never prepared any man or woman for the judgment day.[6] They bind up no broken heart; they heal no wounded conscience. The Greeks had their Zeuxis and Parrhasius, their Phidias and Praxiteles, masters as great in their day as any in modern times; yet the Greeks knew nothing of the way of peace with God. They were sunk in gross idolatry, and bowed down to the works of their own hands.—The most zealous efforts of ministers alone cannot make men Christians. The ablest scriptural reasoning has no effect on

---

[6] 'To wake the soul by tender strokes of art', was the motto which in large letters caught the eye on entering the Manchester Exhibition of Fine Arts, at the extreme end of the building.

the mind; the most fervent pulpit eloquence will not move the heart; the naked truth alone will not lead the will. We who are ministers know this well by painful experience. We can show men the fountain of living waters, but we cannot make them drink. We see many a one sitting under our pulpits year after year, and hearing hundreds of sermons, full of gospel truth, without the slightest result. We mark him year after year, unaffected and unmoved by every scriptural argument,—cold as the stones on which he treads as he enters our church,—unmoved as the marble statue which adorns the tomb against the wall,—dead as the old dry oak of which his pew is made,—feelingless as the painted glass in the windows, through which the sun shines on his head. We look at him with wonder and sorrow, and remember Xavier's words as he looked at China: 'Oh, rock, rock! when wilt thou open?' And we learn by such cases as these, that nothing will make a Christian but the introduction into the heart of a new nature, a new principle, and a divine seed from above.

What is it then that man needs?—We need to be 'born again': and this new birth we must receive of the Holy Ghost. The Spirit of life must quicken us. The Spirit must renew us. The Spirit must take away from us the heart of stone. The Spirit must put in us the heart of flesh. A new act of creation must take place. A new being must be called into existence. Without all this we cannot be saved. Here lies the main part of our need of the Holy Ghost. 'Except a man be born again he cannot see the kingdom of God' (John 3:3). No salvation without a new birth![7]

Let us dismiss from our minds for ever the common idea that natural theology, moral suasion, logical arguments, or even an exhibition of gospel truth, are sufficient of themselves to turn a sinner from his sins, if once brought to bear upon him. It is a strong delusion. They will not do so. The heart of man is far harder than we fancy: the old Adam is much more strong than we suppose. The ships which run aground at half-ebb, will never stir till the tide flows: the heart of man will never look to Christ, repent, and believe, till the Holy Ghost comes down upon it. Till that takes place, our inner nature is like the earth before the present order of creation began,—'without form and void, and darkness covering the face of the deep' (Gen. 1:2). The same power which said at the beginning, 'Let there be light: and there was light,' must work a creating work in us, or we shall never rise to newness of life.

But I have something more to say yet on this branch of my subject. The necessity of the work of the Spirit to man's salvation is a wide field, and I have yet another remark to make upon it.

---

[7] 'This is that which gives unto the ministry of the gospel both its glory and its efficacy. Take away the Spirit from the gospel, and you render it a dead letter, and leave the New Testament of no more use unto Christians than the Old Testament is unto the Jews.'—*Owen on the Holy Spirit.*

'In the power of the Holy Ghost resteth all ability to know God and to please him. It is he that purifieth the mind by his secret working. He enlighteneth the mind to conceive worthy thoughts of Almighty God.'—*Homily for Rogation Week.*

I say then, that without the work of the Holy Ghost *no man could ever be fit to dwell with God in another world*. A fitness of some kind we must have. The mere pardon of our sins would be a worthless gift, unless accompanied by the gift of a new nature, a nature in harmony and in tune with that of God himself. We need a meetness for heaven, as well as a title for heaven, and this meetness we must receive from the Holy Ghost. We must be made 'partakers of the divine nature', by the indwelling of the Holy Ghost (2 Pet. 1:4). The Spirit must sanctify our carnal natures, and make them love spiritual things. The Spirit must wean our affections from things below, and teach us to set them on things above. The Spirit must bend our stubborn wills, and teach them to be submissive to the will of God. The Spirit must write again the law of God on our inward man, and put his fear within us. The Spirit must transform us by the daily renewing of our minds, and implant in us the image of him whose servants we profess to be. Here lies the other great part of our need of the Holy Ghost's work. We need sanctification no less than justification: 'Without holiness no man shall see the Lord' (Heb. 12:14).

Once more I beseech my readers to dismiss from their minds the common idea, that men and women need nothing but pardon and absolution, in order to be prepared to meet God. It is a strong delusion, and one against which I desire with all my heart to place you on your guard. It is not enough, as many a poor ignorant Christian supposes on his deathbed, if God 'pardons our sins and takes us to rest'. I say again most emphatically, it is *not enough*. The love of sin must be taken from us, as well as the guilt of sin removed; the desire of pleasing God must be implanted in us, as well as the fear of God's judgment taken away; a love to holiness must be engrafted, as well as a dread of punishment removed. Heaven itself would be no heaven to us if we entered it without a new heart. An eternal Sabbath and the society of saints and angels could give us no happiness in heaven, unless the love of Sabbaths and of holy company had been first shed abroad in our hearts upon earth.

Whether men will hear or forbear, the man who enters heaven must have the sanctification of the Spirit, as well as the sprinkling of the blood of Jesus Christ. To use the words of Owen, 'When God designed the great and glorious work of recovering fallen man and saving sinners, he appointed in his infinite wisdom two great means. The one was the giving of his Son for them; and the other was the giving of his Spirit unto them. And hereby was way made for the manifestation of the glory of the whole Blessed Trinity.'[8]

I trust I have said enough to show the absolute necessity of the work of the Holy Ghost to the salvation of man's soul. Man's utter inability to turn to God without the Spirit,—man's utter unmeetness for the joys of heaven, without the

[8] 'God the Father had but two grand gifts to bestow; and when once they were given, he had left then nothing that was great (comparatively) to give, for they contained all good in them. These two gifts were his Son, who was his promise in the Old Testament, and the Spirit, the promise of the New.'—*Thomas Goodwin on the Work of the Holy Ghost.* 1704.

Spirit,—are two great foundation stones in revealed religion, which ought to be always deeply rooted in a Christian's mind. Rightly understood, they will lead to one conclusion,—'Without the Spirit, no salvation!'

Would you like to know the reason why we who preach the gospel, preach so often about *conversion*? We do it because of the necessities of men's souls. We do it because we see plainly from the Word of God that nothing short of a thorough change of heart will ever meet the exigencies of your case. Your case is naturally desperate. Your danger is great. You need not only the atonement of Jesus Christ, but the quickening, sanctifying work of the Holy Ghost, to make you a true Christian, and deliver you from hell. Fain would I lead to heaven all who read this volume! My heart's desire and prayer to God is that you may be saved. But I know that none enter heaven without a heart to enjoy heaven, and this heart we must receive from God's Spirit.

Shall I tell you plainly the reason why some receive these truths so coldly, and are so little affected by them? You hear us listless and unconcerned. You think us extreme and extravagant in our statements. And why is this? It is just because you do not see or know the disease of your own soul. You are not aware of your own sinfulness and weakness. Low and inadequate views of your spiritual disease are sure to be accompanied by low and inadequate views of the remedy provided in the gospel. What shall I say to you? I can only say, 'The Lord awaken you! The Lord have mercy on your soul!' The day may come when the scales will fall from your eyes, when old things will pass away, and all things become new. And in that day I foretell and forewarn you confidently that the first truth you will grasp, next to the work of Christ, will be the absolute necessity of the work of the Holy Ghost.

III. The third thing I propose to consider, is *the manner in which the Holy Ghost works on the hearts of those who are saved.*

I approach this branch of my subject with much diffidence. I am very sensible that it is surrounded with difficulties, and involves many of the deepest things of God. But it is folly for mortal man to turn away from any truth in Christianity, merely because of difficulties. Better a thousand times receive with meekness what we cannot fully explain, and believe that what we know not now, we shall know hereafter. 'Enough for us,' says an old divine, 'if we sit in God's court, without pretending to be of God's counsel.'

In speaking of the manner of the Holy Ghost's working, I shall simply state certain great leading facts. They are facts attested alike by Scripture and experience. They are facts patent to the eyes of every candid and well-instructed observer. They are facts which I believe it is impossible to gainsay.

(*a*) I say then that the Holy Ghost works on the heart of a man in a *mysterious manner*. Our Lord Jesus Christ himself tells us that in well-known words,—'The wind bloweth where it listeth, and thou hearest the sound thereof, but canst not tell whence it cometh and whither it goeth; so is every one that is born of the Spirit' (John 3:8). We cannot explain how and in what way the Almighty Spirit comes into man, and operates upon him; but neither also can we explain a thousand things which are continually taking place in the natural world. We cannot explain how our wills work daily on our members, and make them walk, or move, or rest, at our discretion; yet no one ever thinks of disputing the fact. So ought it to be with the work of the Spirit. We ought to believe the fact, though we cannot explain the manner.

(b) I say furthermore, that the Holy Ghost works on the heart of a man in a *sovereign manner*. He comes to one and does not come to another. He often converts one in a family, while others are left alone. There were two thieves crucified with our Lord Jesus Christ on Calvary. They saw the same Saviour dying, and heard the same words come from his lips. Yet only one repented and went to Paradise, while the other died in his sins.—There were many Pharisees besides Saul, who had a hand in Stephen's murder; but Saul alone became an apostle.—There were many slave captains in John Newton's time; yet none but he became a preacher of the gospel.—We cannot account for this. But neither can we account for China being a heathen country, and England a Christian land: we only know that so it is.

(*c*) I say furthermore, that the Holy Ghost always works on the heart of a man in *such a manner as to be felt.* I do not for a moment say that the feelings which he produces are always understood by the person in whom they are produced. On the contrary, they are often a cause of anxiety, and conflict, and inward strife. All I maintain is that we have no warrant of Scripture for supposing that there is an indwelling of the Spirit which is not felt at all. Where he is there will always be corresponding feelings.

(*d*) I say furthermore, that the Holy Ghost always works on the heart of a man in *such a manner as to be seen in the man's life.* I do not say that as soon as he comes into a man, that man becomes immediately an established Christian, a Christian in whose life and ways nothing but spirituality can be observed. But this I say,—that the Almighty Spirit is never present in a person's soul without producing some perceptible results in that person's conduct. He never sleeps: he is never idle. We have no warrant of Scripture for talking of 'dormant grace'. 'Whosoever is born of God doth not commit sin; for his seed remaineth in him' (1 John 3:9). Where the Holy Ghost is, there will be something seen.

(*e*) I say furthermore, that the Holy Ghost always works on the heart of a man in *an irresistible manner.* I do not deny for a moment that there are sometimes spiritual strivings and workings of conscience in the minds of unconverted men, which finally come to nothing. But I say confidently, that when the Spirit really begins a work of conversion, he always carries that work to perfection. He effects miraculous changes. He turns the character upside down. He causes old things to pass away, and all things to become new. In a word, the Holy Ghost is Almighty. With him nothing is impossible.

(*f*) I say, finally, under this head, that the Holy Ghost generally works on the heart of man *through the use of means*. The Word of God, preached or read, is generally employed by him as an instrument in the conversion of a soul. He applies that Word to the conscience. He brings that Word home to the mind. This is his general course of procedure. There are instances, undoubtedly, in which people are converted 'without the word' (1 Pet. 3:1). But, as a general rule, God's truth is the sword of the Spirit. By it he teaches, and teaches nothing else but that which is written in the Word.

I commend these six points to the attention of all my readers. A right understanding of them supplies the best antidote to the many false and specious doctrines by which Satan labours to darken the blessed work of the Spirit.

(*a*) Is there a haughty, high-minded person reading this paper, who in his pride of intellect rejects the work of the Holy Ghost, because of its mysteriousness and sovereignty? I tell you boldly that you must take up other ground than this before you dispute and deny our doctrine. Look to the heaven above you, and the earth beneath you, and deny, if you can, that there are *mysteries* there.—Look to the map of the world you live in, and the marvellous difference between the privileges of one nation and another, and deny if you can, that there is *sovereignty* there.—Go and learn to be consistent. Submit that proud mind of yours to plain undeniable facts. Be clothed with the humility that becomes poor mortal man. Cast off that affectation of reasoning, under which you now try to smother your conscience. Dare to confess that the work of the Spirit may be mysterious and sovereign, and yet for all that is true.

(*b*) Is there a Romanist, or semi-Romanist reading this paper, who tries to persuade himself that all baptized people, and members of the church, as a matter of course, have the Spirit? I tell you plainly that you are deceiving yourself, if you dream that the Spirit is in a man, when his presence cannot be seen. Go and learn this day that the presence of the Holy Ghost is to be tested, not by the name in the register, or the place in the family pew, but by the visible fruits in a man's life.

(*c*) Is there a worldly man reading this paper, who regards all claims to the indwelling of the Spirit as so much enthusiasm and fanaticism? I warn you also to take heed what you are about. No doubt there is plenty of hypocrisy and false profession in the churches; no doubt there are thousands whose religious feelings are mere delusion. But bad money is no proof that there is no such thing as good coin: the abuse of a thing does not destroy the use of it. The Bible tells us plainly that there are certain hopes, and joys, and sorrows, and inward feelings, inseparable from the work of the Spirit of God. Go and learn this day that you have not received the Spirit, if his presence within you has not been felt.

(*d*) Is there an excuse-making indolent person reading this paper, who comforts himself with the thought that decided Christianity is an impossible thing, and that in a world like this he cannot serve Christ? Your excuses will not avail you. The power of the Holy Ghost is offered to you without money and without price. Go and learn this day that there is strength to be had for the asking. Through the Spirit, whom the Lord Jesus offers to give to you, all difficulties may be overcome.

(*e*) Is there a fanatic reading this paper, who fancies that it matters nothing whether a man stays at home or goes to church, and that if a man is to be saved, he will be saved in spite of himself? I tell you also this day, that you have much to learn. Go and learn that the Holy Ghost ordinarily works through the use of means of grace, and that it is by 'hearing' that faith generally comes into the soul (Rom. 10:17).

I leave this branch of my subject here, and pass on. I leave it with a sorrowful conviction that nothing in religion so shows the blindness of natural man as his inability to receive the teaching of Scripture on the manner of the Holy Ghost's operations. To quote the saying of our divine Master,—'The world cannot receive him' (John 14:17). To use the words of Ambrose Serle: 'This operation of the

Spirit hath been, and ever will be, an incomprehensible business to those who have not known it in themselves. Like Nicodemus, and other masters in Israel, they will reason and re-reason, till they puzzle and perplex themselves, by darkening counsel without knowledge; and when they cannot make out the matter, will give the strongest proof of all that they know nothing of it, by fretting and raving, and calling hard names, and saying, in short, that there is no such thing.'

IV. I propose, in the last place, to consider *the marks and evidences by which the presence of the Holy Ghost in a man's heart may be known.*

Last as this point comes in order, it is anything but last in importance. In fact, it is that view of the Holy Ghost which demands the closest attention of every professing Christian. We have seen something of the *place* assigned to the Holy Ghost in the Bible. We have seen something of the absolute *necessity* of the Holy Ghost to a man's salvation. We have seen something of the *manner* of the Holy Ghost's operations. And now comes the mighty question, which ought to interest every reader: 'How are we to know whether we are partakers of the Holy Ghost? By what marks may we find out whether we have the Spirit of Christ?'

I will begin by taking it for granted that the question I have just asked may be answered. Where is the use of our Bibles, if we cannot find out whether we are in the way to heaven? Let it be a settled principle in our Christianity, that a man may know whether or not he has the Holy Ghost. Let us dismiss from our minds once and for ever the many unscriptural evidences of the Spirit's presence with which thousands content themselves. Reception of the sacraments and membership of the visible church are no proofs whatever that we have the Spirit of Christ. In short, I call it a short cut to the grossest Antinomianism to talk of a man having the Holy Ghost so long as he serves sin and the world.

The presence of the Holy Ghost in a man's heart can only be known by the fruits and effects he produces. Mysterious and invisible to mortal eye as his operations are, they always lead to certain visible and tangible results. Just as you know the compass-needle to be magnetized by its turning to the north,—just as you know there is life in a tree by its sap, buds, leaves and fruits,—just as you know there is a steersman on board a ship by its keeping a steady regular course,—just so you may know the Spirit to be in a man's heart by the influence he exercises over his thoughts, affections, opinions, habits, and life. I lay this down broadly and unhesitatingly. I find no safe ground to occupy excepting this. I see no safeguard against the wildest enthusiasm, excepting in this position. And I see it clearly marked out in our Lord Jesus Christ's words: 'Every tree is known by his own fruit' (Luke 6:44).

But what are the specific fruits by which the presence of the Spirit in the heart may be known? I find no difficulty in answering that question. The Holy Ghost always works after a certain definite pattern. Just as the bee always forms the cells of its comb in one regular hexagonal shape, so does the Spirit of God work on the heart of man with one uniform result. His work is the work of a master. The world may see no beauty in it: it is foolishness to the natural man. But 'he that is spiritual discerneth all things' (1 Cor. 2:15). A well-instructed Christian knows well the fruits of the Spirit of God. Let me briefly set them before you in order. They are all clear and unmistakable, 'plain to him that understandeth, and right to them that find knowledge' (Prov. 8:9).

(1) Where the Holy Ghost is, there will always be *deep conviction of sin, and true repentance for it.* It is his special office to convince of sin (John 16:8). He shows the exceeding holiness of God. He teaches the exceeding corruption and infirmity of our nature. He strips us of our blind self-righteousness. He opens our eyes to our awful guilt, folly and danger. He fills the heart with sorrow, contrition, and abhorrence for sin, as the abominable thing which God hateth. He that knows nothing of all this, and saunters carelessly through life, thoughtless about sin, and indifferent and unconcerned about his soul, is a dead man before God. He has not the Spirit of Christ.

(2) Where the Holy Ghost is, there will always be *lively faith in Jesus Christ*, as the only Saviour. It is his special office to testify of Christ, to take of the things of Christ and show them to man (John 16:15). He leads the soul

which feels its sin, to Jesus and the atonement made by his blood. He shows the soul that Christ has suffered for sin, the just for the unjust, to bring us to God. He points out to the sin-sick soul that we have only to receive Christ, believe in Christ, commit ourselves to Christ, and pardon, peace, and life eternal, are at once our own. He makes us see a beautiful fitness in Christ's finished work of redemption to meet our spiritual necessities. He makes us willing to disclaim all merit of our own and to venture all on Jesus, looking to nothing, resting on nothing, trusting in nothing, but Christ,—Christ,—Christ,—'delivered for our offences, and raised again for our justification' (Rom. 4:25). He that knows nothing of all this, and builds on any other foundation, is dead before God. He has not the Spirit of Christ.

(3) Where the Holy Ghost is, there will always be *holiness of life and conversation*. He is the Spirit of holiness (Rom. 1:4). He is the sanctifying Spirit. He takes away the hard, carnal, worldly heart of man, and puts in its place a tender, conscientious, spiritual heart, delighting in the law of God. He makes a man turn his face towards God, and desire above all things to please him, and turn his back on the fashion of this world, and no longer make that fashion his god. He sows in a man's heart the blessed seeds of 'love, joy, meekness, long-suffering, gentleness, goodness, faith, temperance' and causes these seeds to spring up and bear pleasant fruit (Gal. 5:22). He that lacketh these things, and

knows nothing of daily practical godliness, is dead before God. He has not the Spirit of Christ.

(4) Where the Holy Ghost is, there will always be *the habit of earnest private prayer*. He is the Spirit of grace and supplication (Zech. 12:10). He works in the heart as the Spirit of adoption, whereby we cry Abba, Father. He makes a man feel that he must cry to God, and speak to God,— feebly, falteringly, weakly, it may be,—but cry he must about his soul. He makes it as natural to a man to pray as it is to an infant to breathe; with this one difference,—that the infant breathes without an effort, and the new-born soul prays with much conflict and strife. He that knows nothing of real, living, fervent, private prayer, and is content with some old form, or with no prayer at all, is dead before God. He has not the Spirit of Christ.

(5) Finally, where the Holy Ghost is, there will always be *love and reverence for God's Word*. He makes the new-born soul desire the sincere milk of the Word, just as the infant desires its natural food. He makes it 'delight in the law of the Lord' (1 Pet. 2:2; Psa. 1:2). He shows man a fulness, and depth, and wisdom, and sufficiency, in the Holy Scripture, which is utterly hid from a natural man's eyes. He draws him to the Word with an irresistible force, as the light and lantern, and manna, and sword, which are essential to a safe journey through this world. If the man cannot read he makes him love to hear: if he cannot hear he makes him love to meditate. But to the Word the Spirit always leads

him. He that sees no special beauty in God's Bible, and takes no pleasure in reading, hearing, and understanding it, is dead before God. He has not the Spirit of Christ.

I place these five grand marks of the Spirit's presence before my readers, and confidently claim attention to them. I believe they will bear inspection. I am not afraid of their being searched, criticized, and cross-examined. Repentance toward God,—faith toward our Lord Jesus Christ,—holiness of heart and life,—habits of real private prayer,—love and reverence toward God's Word,—these are the real proofs of the indwelling of the Holy Ghost in a man's soul. Where he is, these marks will be seen. Where he is not, these marks will be lacking.

I grant freely that the leadings of the Spirit, in some minute details, are not always uniform. The paths over which he conducts souls, are not always precisely one and the same. The experience that true Christians pass through in their beginnings is often somewhat various. This only I maintain,—that the main road into which the Spirit leads people, and the *final results* which he at length produces, are always alike. In all true Christians, the five great marks I have already mentioned will always be found.

I grant freely that the degree and depth of the work of the Spirit in the heart may vary exceedingly. There is weak faith and strong faith,—weak love and strong love,—bright hope and a dim hope,—a feeble obedience to Christ's will, and a close following of the Lord. This only I maintain,—that the *main outlines* of religious character in all who have the Spirit, perfectly correspond. Life is life, whether strong or feeble. The infant in arms, though weak and dependent, is as real and true a representative of the great family of Adam as the strongest man alive.

Wherever you see these five great marks, you see a true Christian. Let that never be forgotten. I leave it to others to excommunicate and unchurch all who do not belong to their own pale, and do not worship after their own particular fashion. I have no sympathy with such narrow-mindedness. Show me a man who repents, and believes in Christ crucified,—who lives a holy life, and delights in his Bible and prayer,—and I desire to regard him as a brother. I see in him a member of the holy catholic church, out of which there is no salvation. I behold in him an heir of that crown of glory which is incorruptible and fadeth not away. If he has the Holy Ghost, he has Christ. If he has Christ, he has God. If he has God the Father, God the Son, and God the Spirit, all things are his. Who am I that I should turn my back on him, because we cannot see all things eye to eye?

Wherever these five great marks of the Spirit are wanting, we have just cause to be afraid about a man's soul. Visible churches may endorse him, sacraments may be administered to him, forms of prayer may be read over him, ministers may charitably speak of him as 'a brother',—but all this does not alter the real state of things. The man is in the broad way that leadeth to destruction. Without the Spirit he is without Christ. Without Christ he is without God. Without God the Father, God the Son, and God the Spirit, he is in imminent danger. The Lord have mercy upon his soul!

I hasten on now towards a conclusion. I desire to wind up all I have been saying by a few words of direct personal application.

(1) In the first place, let me ask a *question* of all who read this paper. It is a short and simple one, and grows naturally out of the subject. 'Have you, or have you not, the Spirit of Christ?'

I am not afraid to ask this question. I will not be stopped by the commonplace remark that it is absurd, enthusias- tic, unreasonable to ask such questions in the present day. I take my stand on a plain declaration of Scripture. I find an inspired apostle saying, 'If any man have not the Spirit of Christ he is none of his.' I want to know what can be more reasonable than to press on your conscience the inquiry, 'Have you the Spirit of Christ?'

I will not be stopped by the foolish observation, that no man can tell in this world whether or not he has the Spirit. No man can tell! Then what was the Bible given to us for? Where is the use of the Scriptures if we cannot discover whether we are going to heaven or hell? The thing I ask can be known. The evidences of the Spirit's presence in the soul are simple, plain, and intelligible. No honest inquirer needs miss the way in this matter. You may find out whether you have the Holy Ghost.

I entreat you not to evade the question I have now asked. I beseech you to allow it to work inwardly in your heart. I charge you, as ever you would be saved, to give it an honest answer. Baptism, church-membership, respectability, morality, outward correctness, are all excellent things. But do not be content with them. Go deeper: look further. 'Have you received the Holy Ghost? Have you the Spirit of Christ?'[9]

(2) Let me, in the next place, offer a *solemn warning* to all who feel in their own consciences that they have not the Spirit of Christ. That warning is short and simple. If you have not the Spirit, you are not yet Christ's people: you are 'none of his'.

Think for a moment how much is involved in those few words, 'none of his'. You are not washed in Christ's blood! You are not clothed in his righteousness! You are not justified! You are not interceded for! Your sins are yet upon you! The devil claims you for his own! The pit opens her mouth for you! The torments of hell wait for you!

I have no desire to create needless fear. I only want sensible people to look calmly at things as they are. I only want one

[9] 'It is a good sign of grace when a man is willing to search and examine himself, whether he be gracious or not. There is a certain instinct in a child of God, whereby he naturally desires to have the title of his legitimation tried; whereas a hypocrite dreads nothing more than to have his rottenness searched into.'— *Bishop Hopkins.*

plain text of Scripture to be duly weighed. It is written, 'If any man have not the Spirit of Christ, he is none of his.' And I say in the sight of such a text, if you die without the Spirit, you had better never have been born.

(3) Let me, in the next place, give an *earnest invitation* to all who feel that they have not the Spirit. That invitation is short and simple. Go and cry to God this day in the name of the Lord Jesus Christ, and pray for the Holy Spirit to be poured down on your soul.

There is every possible encouragement to do this. There is warrant of Scripture for doing it. 'Turn you at my reproof,—I will pour out my Spirit upon you. I will make known my words unto you.'—'If ye, being evil, know how to give good gifts to your children, how much more shall your heavenly Father give the Holy Spirit to them that ask him' (Prov. 1:23; Luke 11:13). There is warrant in the experience of thousands for doing it. Thousands will rise at the last day, and testify that when they prayed they were heard, and when they sought grace, they found it.—Above all, there is warrant in the Person and character of our Lord Jesus Christ. He waits to be gracious. He invites sinners to come to him. He rejects none that come. He gives 'power to all who receive him by faith and come to him, to become the sons of God' (John 1:12).

Go then to Jesus, as a needy, wanting, humble, contrite sinner, and you shall not go in vain. Cry to him mightily about your soul, and you shall not cry to no purpose. Confess to him your need, and guilt, and fear, and danger, and he will not despise you. Ask, and you shall receive. Seek, and you shall find. Knock, and it shall be opened to you. I testify to the chief of sinners this day, that there is enough in Christ, and to spare, for your soul. Come, come: come, this very day. Come to Christ!

(4) Let me, in the last place, give a parting *word of exhortation* to all readers of this paper who have received the Spirit of Christ,—to the penitent, the believing, the holy, the praying, the lovers of the Word of God. That exhortation shall consist of three simple things.

(*a*) For one thing, be *thankful* for the Spirit. Who has made you to differ? Whence came all these feelings in your heart, which thousands around you know not, and you yourself knew not at one time? To what do you owe that sense of sin, and that drawing towards Christ, and that hunger and thirst after righteousness, and that taste for the Bible and prayer, which, with all your doubts and infirmities, you find within your soul?

Did these things come of nature? Oh, no!—Did you learn these things in the schools of this world? Oh, no: no!—They are all of grace. Grace sowed them, grace watered them, grace began them, grace has kept them up. Learn to be more thankful. Praise God more every day you live: praise him more in private, praise him more in public, praise him in your own family, praise him above all in your own heart.

This is the way to be in tune for heaven. The anthem there will be, 'What hath God wrought?'

(*b*) For another thing, be *filled* with the Spirit. Seek to be more and more under his blessed influence. Strive to have every thought, and word, and action, and habit, brought under obedience to the leadings of the Holy Ghost. Grieve him not by inconsistencies and conformity to the world. Quench him not by trifling with little infirmities and small besetting sins. Seek rather to have him ruling and reigning more completely over you every week that you live. Pray that you may yearly grow in grace, and in the knowledge of Christ. This is the way to do good to the world. An eminent Christian is a North Foreland Lighthouse, seen far and wide by others, and doing good to myriads, whom he never knows.—This is the way to enjoy much inward comfort in this world, to have bright assurance in death, to leave broad evidences behind us, and at last to receive a great crown.

(*c*) Finally, *pray* daily for a great outpouring of the Spirit on the church and on the world. This is the grand want of the day: it is the thing that we need far more than money, machinery, and men. The 'company of preachers' in Christendom is far greater than it was in the days of St Paul; but the actual spiritual work done in the earth, in proportion to the means used, is undoubtedly far less. We want more of the presence of the Holy Ghost,—more in the pulpit, and more in the congregation,—more in the pastoral visit, and more in the school. Where he is, there will be life, health, growth, and fruitfulness. Where he is not, all will be dead, tame, formal, sleepy, and cold. Then let everyone who desires to see an increase of pure and undefiled religion, pray daily for more of the presence of the Holy Ghost in every branch of the visible church of Christ.

Also by J. C. Ryle

Five English Reformers

232pp., paperback
ISBN: 978 0 85151 138 2

Warnings to the Churches

176pp., paperback
ISBN: 978 0 85151 043 9

Thoughts for Young Men

96pp., paperback
ISBN: 978 1 84871 652 0

Also available in
eBook format from our website:

www.banneroftruth.org

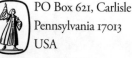